Brazil Apart

By the same author

Passages from Antiquity to Feudalism
Lineages of the Absolutist State

Considerations on Western Marxism
Arguments within English Marxism
In the Tracks of Historical Materialism
The Antinomies of Antonio Gramsci

English Questions
A Zone of Engagement
The Origins of Postmodernity
Spectrum

The New Old World
The Indian Ideology
American Foreign Policy and Its Thinkers
The H-Word

BRAZIL APART
1964–2019

Perry Anderson

VERSO
London • New York

First published by Verso 2019
© Perry Anderson 2019

1 3 5 7 9 10 8 6 4 2

Verso
UK: 6 Meard Street, London W1F 0EG
US: 20 Jay Street, Suite 1010, Brooklyn, NY 11201
versobooks.com

Verso is the imprint of New Left Books

ISBN-13: 978-1-78873-794-4
ISBN-13: 978-1-78873-796-8 (US EBK)
ISBN-13: 978-1-78873-795-1 (UK EBK)

British Library Cataloguing in Publication Data
A catalogue record for this book is available from the British Library

Library of Congress Cataloging-in-Publication Data
A catalog record for this book is available from the Library of Congress

Typeset in Minion Pro by MJ & N Gavan, Truro, Cornwall
Printed and bound by CPI Group (UK) Ltd, Croydon, CR0 4YY

For Roberto and Grecia
&
In memory of Carmute

CONTENTS

FOREWORD

The genesis of this book derives from a larger project, a study of the political life of the major powers of the world, and the emergent inter-state system that they have started to form in the twenty-first century. I began thinking and writing about these in the early nineties; publishing in due course books on Europe and on India.[1] My intention was then to complete the design by bringing together work on the United States, Russia, China and Brazil, of which I had been producing instalments, in a single volume. After finishing the section on Brazil early this year, I was asked by a publisher in São Paulo if it could be translated as a stand-alone book there. On agreeing to this, I came to the conclusion that it made sense to do the same with the original. There were, I decided, both subjective and objective reasons for decanting Brazil from the analytic vessel I previously had in mind.

On the subjective side, my relationship to the country sets it apart in the group of states about which I was writing. Brazil was the first and only foreign country in which I lived—as opposed

---

1   *The New Old World*, Verso 2009; *The Indian Ideology*, Verso 2013.

to visiting—until I was fifty. I was in my twenties, a time when experience is typically more vivid, impressions and connexions go deeper, than in later years. Arriving in Rio in the autumn of 1966, with little knowledge and still less wherewithal to research recent Brazilian history, I returned to London in the spring of 1967, prospects of becoming a Brazilianist lapsing in the student turbulence of 1968. So not a long time to get to know another society. But enough, in this case, to form life-long friendships and fascinations, and a stronger affection for the country, in many ways, than for any other. I was fortunate in the timing of my season in Brazil, for it came in a brief interval between the installation of the military dictatorship in 1964 and its full repressive hardening in 1968, a phase when freedom of speech and print, of screen and stage, had not yet been cancelled, and political opposition could find public expression. In that short-lived interim, the cultural and intellectual energies of the radical ferment which the coup of 1964 intervened to suppress were, if anything, heightened by the electric tensions of resistance to the regime in place. The atmosphere of those months was unforgettable.

When the crack-down of the Fifth Institutional Act of the dictatorship came at the end of 1968, militants taking up arms against it, others driven into exile, memories and contacts remained. Vladimir Herzog, the one Brazilian I knew slightly before going there, who provided me with my only introductions in the country, was tortured and killed by the regime in 1975, his death a watershed in the history of the dictatorship. Among those who escaped, not a few made their way to France. In London, working at *New Left Review*, the Brazilian intellectual colony in Paris was nearby. One of the earliest books this imprint produced was the work of a founder of the VPR guerrillas, today a scholar of Lucretius and Spinoza.[2] The first book to appear in English by Roberto Schwarz, Brazil's foremost literary critic, would come from the same press.[3] Invited to an international conference in Brasília in 1979, I went to the country again soon after exiles were allowed to return, as the dictatorship was preparing its soft landing into a democracy forbidden to investigate its crimes or question its legitimacy. Since then I've gone there often enough, the chapters of this book marking some of the occasions, each of them a political turning-point, when I've done so. What all this has meant is that the forms of my writing on Brazil are sufficiently distinct to warrant separate publication. Texture and tone differ.

On the objective side, Brazil is also a case apart in the gallery of leading states across the world. With the fifth-largest land-mass and population, and now the second-highest per capita income of the BRICs, it is unquestionably a major power, looming larger in its continent than any other in the world except the United States in North America. But history and geography have also made it more isolated and self-contained than any other state of comparable magnitude. In South America, language divides it from every other country. In a region of republics long before Europe achieved these as a norm, it alone formed an empire, lasting nearly a century. Until recent times, dense rainforest, desolate scrub and impassable marsh separated its vast interior from every neighbouring state save on its narrow southernmost border. Culturally and psychologically, Brazilian society in large measure turned its back on the Hispanic world surrounding it to the west, looking away to Europe, and latterly up to the United States. But the South Atlantic is a long way from the North

---

2   João Quartim, *Dictatorship and Armed Struggle in Brazil*, Verso 1971.
3   Roberto Schwarz, *Misplaced Ideas*, Verso 1992.

Atlantic, and a geopolitical vacuum whose other shores have figured only as the source of slaves in the Brazilian past. Not even Portugal registers much in Brazil's contemporary imagination or connexion; far less than Spain for its onetime colonies, from where so many leading writers have decamped to Madrid or Barcelona.[4] The result is a national culture that remains, among its peers in the ranks of major powers, uniquely self-contained: without the links to its neighbours of a common Confucian past, in China; of the English language to the Anglosphere, in India; of centuries of intellectual and diplomatic interchange with Europe, in Russia; of the intimacy of Cold War bonding with the United States, in Europe. Only the US, behind its ocean moats and conviction of divine preference, approaches Brazil in its degree of introversion; in its case, however, leavened by immigrants from all over the world. Brazil too benefited greatly from these between the wars, who contributed much to its culture after them; but they have since ceased to arrive, sealing its enclosure. In no other nation-state today is there such unself-conscious thought of the country as a civilization entire unto itself—the locution *a civilização brasileira* by no means just a boastful appanage of the right, but a spontaneous expression of historians and publicists across the political spectrum to the left.[5] This has

---

4   The relative sizes of former colony and former metropole have, of course, something to do with this Ibero-American contrast. Still, in a period when a society of over 200 million could scarcely boast of a poet or a novelist to compare with Pessoa or Saramago, products of a society of less than 10 million, the lack of interest in Portugal of even the most educated Brazilians is often striking.

5   In France, if *la civilisation française* was once a hallowed expression, it is now a deflated anachronism. Not so in Brazil. In 1960, when Sérgio Buarque de Holanda, the doyen of the country's modern historiography and a figure of the socialist left, launched what would become the eleven volumes (the first is now in its seventeenth edition) of the *História Geral*

not meant provincialism, in any ordinary sense of the word. The country forms too big a universe on its own, in which any number of creative minds can find full absorption with its own problems, without need to look much farther afield, for that. But a national culture that remains so largely sufficient to itself as the natural horizon of thought is, for better or worse, not unlike a nineteenth-century exception in this one.

A further, politically more decisive, determinant separates Brazil from its peers in the Northern hemisphere. It is a major but not a Great Power, since it does not possess the armed force—sheer military weight: troops, tanks, carriers, aircraft, missiles—which continues to define that status, and would qualify it for the rank. Under their own flags, all the other contenders for it have fought wars since 1945: China in Korea, India and Vietnam; Russia in Afghanistan and the Caucasus; Europe in the Balkans and Middle East; India in Bengal, Ceylon and Kashmir; the United States in the Far East, the Middle East, the Balkans, North Africa and the Caribbean. Brazil has not. Its army is puny compared with the might of these states. On the other hand, unlike in

---

da Civilização Brasileira in 1960, he remarked disarmingly that while in other circumstances the title might seem inappropriate or presumptuous, it was natural enough in taking its cue from a translation from the French of Maurice Crouzet's *Histoire générale des civilisations* by the same publisher, Difel. In reality, the expression did not depend on this artifice. It was current much earlier. The publishing house Civilização Brasileira was founded in 1929, among its trio of founders Gustavo Barroso, later the most prolific theorist of Integralismo on the fascist right. In 1934, when the University of São Paulo was created under Vargas, the history department included a chair of 'Brazilian Civilization' from the start, its first principal occupant a conservative liberal, Alfredo Ellis, whom Sergio Buarque succeeded in 1956 as holder of the chair. By that time Ênio Silveira, a communist, had taken over the publishing house Civilização Brasileira, creating in the mid sixties an important review of the combative left with the same name, closed down by the dictatorship in 1968.

any of them, it constitutes a central political power within the country. What it lacks in external throw-weight, it makes up for in domestic strike-capacity. Not aggression abroad, but repression at home has been its great vocation. This is the configuration which frames the period explored in the pages to come.

For in these years, Brazil was also the theatre of a socio-political drama without equivalent in any other major state. Everywhere else—in Europe, the United States, India, Russia, China—the trend of the times was towards a tightening of the grip of the rich over the poor, of capital over labour, and a widen-ing of the gulf between them, in state and society: oligarchy in one form or another, neo-liberal or hybrid. In Brazil alone, there was for a time a movement in the other direction. The dozen years of rule by the Workers' Party made Brazil, for the first time in its modern history, a country that mattered politically beyond its borders, as an example and potential inspiration to others. Not by accident for the first time too, a power that could play an independent role on the international stage. Neither at home nor abroad was performance ever unblemished. The limitations of what was attempted, and weaknesses of what was accomplished, are part of the account. But that it came to an end in the way that it did speaks for it, as well as against it: evidence that whatever else the PT in office had become, the degree of its departure from the rules of the period was insupportable to the traditional powers of the land. In 1964–68 one government judged too radical was overthrown by a military coup, install-ing a dictatorship. Half a century later, in 2016–18 another was overthrown by a parliamentary coup, installing a fervent admirer of the dictatorship in the presidency. In his government, there are now more military ministers than there were under the rule of the generals. The situation, and the regime, are not the same.

But that the overall curve of history, from the beginning to the end of these fifty years, forms a parabola—one which gives its shape to the narrative, and title to the conclusion, of what follows—is plain.

I could and would never have written on Brazil without the conversation, advice and in many cases friendship, of those with whom I talked about the country over the years. Inexhaustively, but in particular: Maria do Carmo Campello de Souza, Mario Sergio Conti, Edgard Carone, Roberto Fragale, Elio Gaspari, Marcus Giraldes, Eduardo Kugelmas, Lena Lavinas, Roberto Mangabeira Unger, Leôncio Martins Rodrigues, Conrado Hübner Mendes, Juliana Neuenschwander, Chico de Oliveira, Leda Paulani, Paulo Sérgio Pinheiro, Marcio Pochmann, Emir Sader, André Singer, Luiz Eduardo Soares, Roberto Schwarz, Pedro Paulo Zahluth Bastos. None would have agreed with everything, in some cases perhaps anything, I've written about Brazil. But I learnt from all of them. None more than from my oldest friend in São Paulo, Roberto Schwarz, a literary critic whose political judgment stands by itself in his generation. Responsibility for errors is mine alone.

The first versions of chapters 1–5 appeared in the *London Review of Books* respectively on 24 November 1994; 12 December 2002; 31 March 2011; 21 April 2016; and 7 February 2019. Where they contain changes of opinion, as later events threw fresh light on earlier ones, I have left these unaltered, as part of the record; so too, overlaps in the narrative. The date below the title of each chapter refers to the time of its composition.

LAUNCH

1994

Brazil today has a larger population and gross national product than Russia. Yet, against all reason, it continues to occupy a curiously marginal position in the contemporary historical imaginary. In fifteen years it has left virtually no trace in the pages of the *London Review*. Popular images, despite increasing tourism, remain scanty: folk-villains on the run, seasonal parades in fancy-dress, periodical football triumphs. In cultural influence, while the music and literature of Latin America have swept round the world, Brazil has receded. The rhythms of salsa have long eclipsed those of the samba, and the list of headline novelists conspicuously omits the country that produced the most inventive nineteenth-century practitioner of the form outside Europe, in Machado de Assis. Today Northern readers are more likely to get an impression of the country from Peruvian bombast than any native fiction.

If the largest society in the Southern hemisphere remains mentally off-screen for most outsiders, part of the reason lies in its recent political history. Since the sixties, there have been four major dramas in Latin America that have caught the attention of the world. Three of these were either by-passed or aborted in Brazil, and the other took a *sui generis* form. Internationally, the continent became news for the first time in the wake of the Cuban Revolution, when the spectre of guerrilla movements haunted Washington. Brazil was never in the forefront of this turbulence. Compared with Venezuela or Colombia, Peru or Argentina, its episodes of insurgency—largely urban—were brief and soon extinguished. Military dictatorship, on the other hand, arrived earlier—already in 1964, nearly a decade before Pinochet or Videla—and lasted longer, for over twenty years. The Brazilian generals were always the most adroit of the region, presiding over record rates of growth in the seventies, and opening a carefully calibrated re-democratization in the eighties, in a process whose outcome they controlled nearly to the end.

In 1984 huge demonstrations for direct elections broke out in the big cities, as a domesticated Congress prepared to pick a new president, under guidelines from the High Command. The regime did not yield. But fear of popular retribution split the civilian elites that had hitherto supported it, as many of the landed notables of the North-East—the core of its system of political alliances—defected to the opposition. The military held off the pressure from the streets, but at the cost of losing control of Congress, where a 'liberal front' of retrograde landowners and local bosses, hitherto pliable henchmen of the regime, switched from the official candidate to a moderate politician, Tancredo Neves, running as a symbol of constitutional principle and reconciliation.

Although Neves had never been an especially outspoken opponent of the dictatorship, and would not have won a competition under direct elections, his indirect adoption by Congress as the new president was nevertheless consecrated by public opinion, amidst enormous expectation, as the final victory of democracy over praetorian tyranny. His sudden death on the eve of his inauguration punctured all euphoria. The new president became instead a leading ornament of the dictatorship: José Sarney, a belle-lettrist oligarch from the latifundia of Maranhão, whom Neves had chosen as his running-mate to clinch the support of last-minute defectors from the regime in the North-East. The ideological anti-climax was acute. Brazil shuffled into the era of democratization, common to Latin America, bewildered and dispirited. There was no sharp discontinuity of institutions or persons, comparable to the fall of the junta in Argentina or the rejection of autocracy in Chile.

Trying to make good his lack of popular legitimacy, Sarney formed a government that was actually somewhat less conservative than the administration envisaged by Neves—a characteristic Brazilian move. But his presidency remained weak and erratic. When he came in, annual inflation was running at over 200 per cent; when he went out, a series of misfired shock treatments and emergency plans left it rising towards 2,000 per cent. The late eighties were a time of economic recession and growing social tension. In 1988 a new Constitution was adopted, with more democratic safeguards than hitherto, but otherwise an unwieldy and incoherent charter. When the first direct elections for president were held under it in 1989, the result was a tight contest between the Left, represented by Lula—Luiz Inácio da Silva, former auto-worker and trade-union leader—and the Right, in the shape of a playboy demagogue from one of the oldest and richest political families in the country, Fernando Collor de Mello. With stentorian backing from the Globo television empire, commanding 70 per cent of all viewers, and charismatic appeal to the unorganized poor, Collor won by a narrow margin. His inaugural address—drafted by José Guilherme Merquior, the most talented liberal intellectual of his generation, well-known as a diplomat in London—promised a sweeping demolition of state controls, and release of the spirit of freedom and individual enterprise, with due concern for the least advantaged. The hour of Latin American neo-liberalism, chiming in with the arrival of Salinas in Mexico, Menem in Argentina and Fujimori in Peru, seemed now to have arrived in Brazil.

But once more, the typical experience of the continent short-circuited. Collor did start to reduce tariffs, privatize public companies and cut bureaucratic payrolls. But his bid to beat down inflation by freezing bank deposits proved even more chaotic than Sarney's efforts, antagonizing the well-off without achieving any stabilization. Then a family quarrel in his fief of Alagoas suddenly revealed a trail of monumental malfeasance, even by tolerant local standards: slush-funds of $200 million, extorted for political clientage and personal ostentation. Since Collor had based his electoral campaign on promises to root out corruption, such brazen looting stunned even close followers. As the charges mounted, Collor went on television and called the people to demonstrate their patriotic support for the president in his battle against an elite conspiracy by sporting the green and yellow colours of the nation. The next day the cities were decked in black. Within six weeks he was out of office. If democratization in Brazil had issued into ambiguity and confusion, liberalization ended in farce. By 1992, when Collor was ejected, the country appeared to have missed the trend of the times once again. While Argentina, Uruguay, Chile, Peru, Mexico, were posting much-touted economic recoveries under neo-liberal discipline, Brazil was still floundering in an inflationary morass, apparently rudderless.

Two years later, the scene suddenly looks different. In and through the inflationary spiral of the past decade, and the deep recessions of 1981 to '83 and subsequently, the Brazilian economy continued to diversify. Unobtrusively, capital stock was modernized, productivity rose, and exports increased, from about $3–4 billion a year in 1981 to some $25 billion in 1994, yielding a positive trade balance and substantial reserves. By the mid nineties, the objective weight of the country in the new global order had altered. Richer and more orderly than Yeltsin's Federation, Brazil is within sight of achieving the rank of a major power, to which it never—despite much over-blown rhetoric—came near in the past; and for the first time in its history, the country has acquired a ruler capable of putting it unmistakably on the international map. Fernando Henrique Cardoso, when he becomes president next year, will arguably be the most intellectually sophisticated head of any state in the world.

In Latin America, from the time of Sarmiento or Nabuco onwards, writers and scholars have traditionally played a major role on the political stage. Vargas Llosa's ambition to govern Peru is a recent episode. Rómulo Gallegos, another novelist, was Venezuela's first elected president after the war. The current foreign minister of Argentina, Guido di Tella, a distinguished economic historian, is a long-time fellow of St Anthony's, Oxford. In that sense, Cardoso, co-author with Enzo Faletto of the most influential single work of South American social science in the sixties—*Dependency and Development in Latin America*—fits a regional pattern. His rise to power even has a wryly appropriate national touch. Brazil was the only country in the world where the inventor of sociology as a discipline, Auguste Comte, inspired the founders of the Republic, firing young officers to overthrow the Empire in 1889 and bequeathing the motto—*Ordem e Progresso*—that still unfurls across the national flag. A century later, on the same soil, Comte's dream of the sociologist-ruler has come true.

There is, however, more than one irony in its fulfilment, for the kind of sociology that made Cardoso's name was the antithesis of positivism. His work represented a Marxism whose point of honour was a dialectical understanding of society. In the Latin America of the sixties and seventies, that might seem commonplace. In fact, however, it emerged from an exceptional milieu, which is the key to Cardoso's early career. He was the son of a nationalist general at a time when the Brazilian officer corps was sharply divided between anti-communist and left-nationalist factions. In the early fifties he studied at the University of São Paulo, where he soon got a teaching post. At that time—this is not something the Brazilian press, protective of the presidential candidate, cared to mention till after the elections—he was effectively a Communist. The PCB was then the only significant organization of the Brazilian Left, so there was little unusual about the choice. He moved away from the party in 1956, but for a good many years remained informally close to it—part of the *linha auxiliar*, as such sympathizers were called. More formative than this affiliation, however, was the institution at which he worked.

The University of São Paulo was founded in 1934 by a group of liberal oligarchs, led by the scion of the city's newspaper dynasty, Júlio de Mesquita Filho. At the time German and Italian cultural influence was strong in Brazil—reflecting not only the importance of the two immigrant communities, but also the growing prestige of European fascism, which was to inspire the creation of the authoritarian *Estado Novo* by Getúlio Vargas three years later. The *paulista* liberals, resolved to create an institution with high intellectual standards, wanted European lecturers for it. For mathematics, natural sciences and classics they were willing to engage Italians and Germans. But for the social sciences and philosophy, where political issues were at stake, they contracted with the French state, whose teachers—they felt—could be relied on to uphold democratic values. The arrangement bore historic fruit in the series of great French names who, before they were known in the world at large, came to the Faculty in São Paulo: Claude Lévi-Strauss, Fernand Braudel, Pierre Monbeig, Roger Bastide, Claude Lefort, Michel Foucault. The deepest local imprint was left in philosophy, where a set of outstanding instructors trained a generation of thinkers, vividly memorialized in a recent work by Paulo Eduardo Arantes as *Um Departamento Francês de Ultramar*. By the late fifties this was an intellectual milieu—not unexpectedly—increasingly interested in Marx. In 1958 a group of young intellectuals from different disciplines—it included Cardoso from sociology, Paul Singer from economics, José Arthur Giannotti from philosophy, Roberto Schwarz from literature—started a seminar on *Capital* that became a legend, lasting five years and affecting the atmosphere of the Faculty for ten.

When the Armed Forces seized power in 1964, the immediate targets of proscription were mainly politicians, or those close to them. With a military search out for him, Cardoso chose flight to Chile. In the university, most of his colleagues continued to work relatively unmolested. In these years, when the dictatorship had radicalized intellectual opposition without yet repressing it, the Faculty on Rua Maria Antônia was an unforgettable place. An inconspicuous, squat building near the centre of the city, with a dingy façade and lugubrious interior, surrounded by a tangle of bars and *lanchonetes* into which its life continuously spilt out, it was like some magical cave of—mostly political—ideas and passions. The French connexion was still active: certainly, for anyone coming from London, the scene had elements of a tropical version of the *sixième*. But it was also in many ways livelier. Intellectually, the Faculty seminar on *Capital* predated the famous one at the École Normale. Here in São Paulo—it came as a shock to discover in 1966—there already existed a study of the Feuerbachian matrix of the young Marx, much more scholarly than any published by the Althusserian school, in Giannotti's *Origens da Dialéctica do Trabalho*. The Marxism of the Maria Antônia was also more cosmopolitan than that of the Rue d'Ulm: the Frankfurt School, still a blank page in Paris, was a significant presence, as were Austro-Marxist traditions. All this mingled with the incomparable Brazilian sociability; the flow of equatorial *batidas* over the tiny counters; the enigma of women more independent than in Europe, emancipated by maids; an electric sense of upheavals to come. For the visiting student, a heady brew.

By 1968 political opposition to the dictatorship was mounting: parliamentary manoeuvres, industrial strikes, university rebellions, even scattered armed actions. In October a pitched battle broke out between students of Mackenzie College, the conservative private university on the other side of the Maria Antônia, opposite the Faculty building, and militants at the USP. Bombarded by the superior forces of the Right, the Faculty was burnt out, and one of its defenders killed—whereupon the army sent in the cavalry and closed the site permanently, bringing an era to an end. A few weeks later, the regime clamped down much more toughly than in 1964, with the Fifth Institutional Act that clinched its power for the next decade. Cardoso, who had returned

to Brazil a few months earlier, was forcibly removed from the chair
to which he had just been elected at the Faculty. But he had used
his years abroad to good advantage, and with funding from the
Ford Foundation helped set up a research centre in Sao Paulo,
CEBRAP, that would later carry on much of the spirit of the Maria
Antônia, in collective investigations of Brazilian society under the
dictatorship. In this period, the dominant influence in his thought
continued to be Marxist. In the early seventies, while pursuing empirical work, Cardoso was doing battle with Poulantzas
over the definition of social classes, clarifying uses or misuses
of the category of dependency, of a reserve army of labour, of
marginality. A decade later, he was asking whether Gramsci's
concept of hegemony could still be valid when 'liberal-democratic
parliamentarism is disappearing as a principle of legitimacy in
advanced societies themselves': new forms of 'state-bourgeois'
domination required, for the fight against them, the invention of
new forms of 'control of production', respectful of initiatives and
liberties, in the articulation of a 'socialist utopia'.[1]

In the mid seventies the military regime, confident that the
country was now secured against subversion, started its slow
institutional opening. As soon as it did so, the opposition party
which it had itself created—the MDB—rapidly gained ground,
as a united front against the dictatorship. In 1978 Cardoso ran
for Senator on a sub-section of its ticket in São Paulo. He was
uncomfortable on the hustings, and easily defeated. But he
came in second, and so under a recent military law remained
suplente—'next in line'—behind the successful candidate. Four
years later, when the Senator was in turn elected Governor, the

---

1   Fernando Henrique Cardoso, 'Political Regime and Social Change: Some
Reflections on the Brazilian Case', *Stanford-Berkeley Occasional Papers in
Latin American Studies*, No 3, Fall 1981, pp. 20–2.

substitute slipped into his vacant seat. It was a privileged entry into the world of high politics. He still had much to learn. In 1985, while still Senator, he ran for Mayor of São Paulo. Posing over-confidently for photographers in City Hall on the eve of the polls, he provoked a reaction and lost. The next year, however, there were new congressional elections. By now the omnibus party of which he had become a fixture, the PMDB, was no longer in opposition: it was the official base of President Sarney, whose Cruzado Plan—apparently quelling inflation with the issue of a new currency a few months before the election—gave it a landslide throughout the country, carrying Cardoso with a large margin back into the Senate.

Once the elections were over, the Cruzado Plan collapsed. Sarney lost all credit, and the PMDB—never more than a loose patchwork—came apart at the seams. In 1988 Cardoso, now president of the Senate, and a group of colleagues seceded from it to found the Brazilian Social-Democratic Party (PSDB). In his case, the move crystallized a political evolution. Within the PMDB, a catch-all front stretching from undeclared Communists to scarcely repentant collaborationists, ideological positions typically remained veiled or indeterminate. Over time, however, Cardoso came to favour with increasing clarity a political strategy close to that of Eurosocialism. The aim of the PSDB was to become a Brazilian version of the parties of González or Mitterrand. Initially, the project of a modernist social-democracy looked fragile. In the first round of the presidential election of 1989, the party's candidate was easily outpolled by two rivals to its left, not only the radical trade-unionist Lula, running for the Workers' Party (PT), but also the veteran populist Brizola. On the second ballot, after some hesitation, it backed Lula against Collor. But many of its voters—especially in São Paulo, where the electoral balance was critical—opted for Collor, helping him to victory.

The new president, catapulted into office through television, lacked any organized base in Congress. To start with, he tried to govern the country with a motley group of personal appointees, often amateurs without party background. But when these utterly failed to bring inflation under control, Collor changed tack and tried to draw politicians of some weight into his government. The PSDB was among the parties to which he made overtures. Invited to take office under Collor, its leadership divided. Cardoso was among those who favoured joining his Cabinet. A month later, the scandal of presidential corruption—already bubbling—boiled over. Once Congress had formally set up an enquiry, Collor became a political untouchable. This was a narrow escape for Cardoso. Had the investigation not started so quickly, he would have paid a stiff price for his willingness to work with Collor. In the subsequent congressional investigation, the PSDB did not play a leading part: success in exposing the president fell principally to the PT.

But by a strange twist, Collor's impeachment gave Cardoso his breakthrough. Collor had picked a small-town politician from the backlands of Minas for his running-mate, with whom he had nothing in common, and completely ignored as vice-president. This individual, Itamar Franco, was now suddenly put, blinking with bewilderment, into the Presidential Palace. A pale, shapeless figure, he had never aspired to supreme office and few ideas what to do with it, although his instincts were humane and he was honest. Timid and provincial, he desperately needed counsel and reassurance. The PSDB came forward to help him, and he made Cardoso foreign minister. Soon he was captivated. Fernando Henrique—from this point we may drop the surname, as Brazilians now do—was everything Itamar was not. Strikingly good-looking, he combines a natural authority with an urbane charm whose flickering smile does not mask, but conveys inner reserve and strength of purpose. Within a few months, this cosmopolitan prince enjoyed an ascendancy over an awkward, nervous ruler more reminiscent of the position of a court favourite like a Buckingham or Godoy than of a member of a modern cabinet.

In the spring of 1993 Itamar gave him the most powerful job in the government, the Ministry of Finance. Inflation was still raging at a rate exceeded only by Serbia and Zaire. At the Ministry, Fernando Henrique assembled a group of gifted economists, long-time friends, who prepared yet another stabilization plan. This time it was a technically competent scheme, that did not rely on price controls that no Brazilian government has the power to enforce, achieved real cuts in public spending, and was phased in gradually, rather than decreed overnight. Crucially, there also for the first time existed substantial foreign reserves, capable of backing a hard currency. The initial measures, involving labyrinthine bargaining in Congress, were not dramatic. While they were being negotiated, the public mood was swinging rapidly against the government. Outside the hothouse of Brasília, popular disaffection with the political establishment was running high. The destruction of Collor and the interim of Itamar had left a political vacuum, in which only one oppositional force looked credible. This was the party headed by Lula.

The origins of the PT lay in the metal-workers' strikes that had erupted in the industrial belt round São Paulo in the late seventies. There Lula rose to fame as a trade union leader in the same year Fernando Henrique (ten years older) first ran for

Congress. The two were then allies. Out of the new working-class militancy, however, emerged a grass-roots determination to create a political party that would not be a new edition of traditional left populism, and could not be absorbed into the capacious folds of the PMDB. The aim of the PT, founded in 1980, was to develop an independent politics of labour in Brazil. Since its primary impulse came from a rebellious trade-union movement, and much of its social inspiration from base communities in the Catholic Church, it was often compared to Solidarity—an analogy of which it was proud; although there was always a third component in the party, absent in Poland, supplied by a Marxist Left that had broken with Stalinism. Initially, the performance of the PT at the polls was quite modest: by 1986 it still attracted only 7 per cent of the electorate. Three years later, however, the size of the asset it possessed in its leader became apparent. Lula, who comes from a peasant family in the North-East that migrated to São Paulo, where he got a job in a nuts-and-bolts factory at the age of thirteen, is an authentic working-class hero—unschooled and unpretentious, a courageous organizer and a passionate speaker: a man with whom millions of the excluded could identify. In 1989, his second place in the first round of the presidential elections was an impressive advance, but still only represented 16 per cent of the poll. It was the second ballot against Collor, when he pulled in 43 per cent of the voters behind him, that established Lula as a national politician with an appeal capable of extending well beyond his own party.

Two years later the downfall of Collor, in which the PT played a prominent role, inevitably spot-lit the opponent who had nearly defeated him. By May of this year, with presidential elections set for October, Lula had built up what appeared to many an unassailable lead in the opinion polls—over 40 per cent.

Fernando Henrique, who had just stepped down as minister to run against him, was the preference of no more than some 16 per cent of the voters. Five months later, the outcome was the reverse. In October Fernando Henrique trounced Lula by a huge margin—54 to 27 per cent. What caused this stunning turn-around? First, and most fundamentally, the success of the new currency—the *real*—which replaced the discredited *cruzado* in June. The impact of the change was instantaneous, just as that of the *cruzado* itself had once been. Within the space of eight weeks, inflation fell from 47.2 to 1.5 per cent. In the rich countries, we are accustomed to the fine-tuning of economic policies to the electoral cycle—the loosening of credit or the lowering of taxes for political advantage in the run-up to polls. But the margin of advantage such adjustments yield incumbents bears no comparison with the rewards of suddenly stabilizing money in a developing country gripped by hyper-inflation.

On the eve of the reform, no economy in the world was so indexed as that of Brazil. First introduced by the dictatorship in the sixties to encourage long-term holding of government bonds, the principle of proofing assets and incomes against inflation by ever more complicated and pervasive systems of adjustment spread remorselessly as inflation took off in the late seventies. Eventually, any ordinary bank account was theoretically insulated against the monthly spiral of price increases by these devices. This was one of the factors that made inflation in Brazil so durable and also relatively tolerable. Protection, however, extended only to those with significant savings—the upper and middle classes who make up less than a third of the population. For the poor, dependent on precarious sources of cash, money lost its value at terrifying speed: wages had to be spent in a day if they were not to lose half their purchasing power by the end of the month. Here the acceleration of the monetary whirligig was nightmarish. To be able to halt it, even temporarily, is—because the immediate relief is so tangible, in every transaction of daily life—the political equivalent of a grand slam.

The introduction of the *real* was, of course, hailed by Brazilian business and banking as a restoration of sound money and financial orthodoxy, and welcomed as a simplification of existence by the middle classes. But it was the least well-off, the great majority of ordinary people, who were most immediately affected. Its timing, carefully premeditated, was perfect. Had the new currency been launched earlier, there was the danger of it unravelling under the pressures that had overwhelmed previous attempts to disinflate the Brazilian economy. Had it been delayed till later, as rigorists in the technical group which prepared the *Plano Real* wanted, it would have deprived the minister of the thunderbolt that transformed his candidacy. The PT, whose electoral platform had scarcely mentioned the problem of inflation, was caught off-guard and lacked any credible alternative.

The *real* was in itself probably enough to assure Fernando Henrique of victory: within a month of its introduction, he was well ahead of Lula. But he had not quite believed in such a miraculous effect himself, and had taken out an insurance policy. Before the new currency came into force, he concluded an alliance with the leading political cartel of the North-Eastern oligarchy, the 'Liberal Front' (PFL) which had abandoned the dictatorship at the last minute, after its members had adorned it for twenty years. The region over which this class presides is another world from the industrial South-Centre of the country— one of misery, hunger, and disease, social despair and early death. Traditional landowners, controlling vast ill-run estates, form the core of the ruling stratum here. But under the military regime and its postlude, when Sarney held the presidency, lavish patronage from Brasília financed the commercial modernization of state capitals, spawning new outworks for the local dynasties —the Collor empire in Alagoas was a case in point—and a technically sleeker generation of notables.

In this region, the means of political power have increasingly shifted from the bailiff towards broadcasting—no self-respecting clan is now without its radio or TV station. But the substance remains much the same. In the late sixties, this was a Namieresque landscape of families like the Rosado connexion in Rio Grande do Norte, so numerous that its patriarch ran out of names for his last-born, simply enumerating them—a touch of elegance—in French: there were two Congressmen called, respectively, Dix-Huit and Vingt Rosado. Today, nearly half the entire congressional delegation of the (large) state of Pará are relatives of the former Governor (now incumbent Senator). The politician from the Liberal Front chosen by Cardoso to be his running-mate, Marco Maciel, henchman of the military in the seventies, is the fifth of his line to have governed Pernambuco since the 1820s.

Why did Fernando Henrique make this alliance, to the shock of many admirers? The electoral clientele of the PFL was one reason. Its network of local bosses could deliver a secure package of votes, which few other potential partners could match. But there was also a wider calculation. A deal with the PFL sent a signal to all sectors of the Brazilian establishment that Fernando Henrique could be trusted as a barrier against Lula. Some of these were much more powerful than any regional clan in the North-East. Above all, in Rio there was the *Globo* empire of the newspaper magnate Roberto Marinho, a stout champion of the dictatorship, who had gained an impregnable dominance of television under it. In those days the minister responsible for awarding the crucial licenses was Antônio Carlos Magalhães, of the Bahía oligarchy, later the most important architect of the PFL. No-one was better placed to broker the adoption of Fernando Henrique by the *Globo* machine. Once Marinho, who had so largely elected Collor, was convinced, the full force of a television chain whose standards resemble those of Murdoch or Berlusconi, swung into action. The more decorous organs of business and establishment opinion, from the conservative *Estado de S. Paulo* of the Mesquita family downwards, followed suit.

Queried about these allies at a press conference, Fernando Henrique philosophically remarked: 'People change. Politics is about transformation. Nobody can govern a country of the size of Brazil without alliances. If we're talking about those who supported the military regime, there weren't two hundred individuals who had the courage to struggle against the dictatorship. You can't make a government with two hundred persons.'[2] In reality, of course, there were thousands who had resisted the dictatorship. The tacit reference could only be to the natural rulers of the country. Perhaps the second sentence is the most pregnant. It looks anodyne to the point of vacancy, unlikely in this mind. But it is not without resonance. Should we hear behind 'transformation' the echo of a delicate cognate? The Italian term *trasformismo* refers to the political process—inveterate in its country of origin—whereby radical pressures are gradually absorbed and inverted by conservative forces, until they serve the opposite of their original ends. Lampedusa coined its most expressive maxim.

But if in Italy *trasformismo* has generally connoted an

---

2   Assertions repeated on a number of occasions: e.g. 'FHC culpa PDT e PT por data do Real', *Folha*, 29 September 1994.

organic, molecular alteration—of a kind which leaves all that is essential unaltered—analogous shifts in Latin America are altogether more precipitous and volatile. This is the continent *par excellence* of sudden political reconciliations and ideological volte-faces. In neighbouring Bolivia, the MIR—'Movement of the Revolutonary Left'—a few years ago joined forces with General Banzer, former dictator of the Right, in a coalition to thwart a discredited Centre. Fernando Henrique's deal with the PFL is in this pragmatic tradition. But in Brazil such switches of alliance, often no less startling than elsewhere, are typically less brittle. The dark side of Brazilian conviviality is the ease with which instrumental calculation becomes sentimental affinity, binding opposites together in subtler and more durable forms of union. Which side tends to transform which, in such amalgams, is not difficult to guess. Historically, Brazilian conservatism has been uniquely ductile in its capacity to embrace and disarm risks to the status quo.

For the moment, however, the pact with the Right has paid off. By August it was obvious that, armed with the impact of the new money, the alliance of the old elite and the support of the mass media, Fernando Henrique was unbeatable. The campaign itself was a one-sided affair. A month before polling, the finance minister put in to manage the *Plano Real*—presidential candidates must resign office once they have declared—was caught by parabolic antennae telling a television interviewer, off the record, that he was manipulating price statistics to boost Cardoso's claim to have defeated inflation. 'I have no scruples', Rubens Ricupero confided. 'What is good news we exploit; what is bad we hide.' He continued: 'As Fernando Henrique knows, I am his great elector. This is terrific for the *Globo* network. Instead of having to give him any ostentatious support, they can put me on the air and no-one can make any objection. This is what we might call an indirect solution, heh?"[3] Government intervention in favour of any presidential candidate is specifically forbidden by the new constitution, so this was a boast not just of deception but illegality. In most countries it is difficult to imagine a candidate easily surviving such an indiscretion. In Brazil too, had Lula been associated with a scandal like this, he would no doubt have paid for it. But with steadily benevolent media, and largely uneducated voters, it caused scarcely a ripple in Fernando Henrique's progress towards victory. When asked by pollsters, half of the electorate didn't know what the word 'scruple' meant.

Culturally, the gulf between the privileged and the *povão*—the broad mass of the population—might have been expected to favour Lula, as a son of the poor and unlettered. In fact, its effect was the opposite. The stocky, bearded figure winding up audiences on the stump, hoarse with fatigue and emotion, won over fewer of the disadvantaged than the coolly elegant authority setting out priorities for the nation, in television spots as technically polished as any up north (professional advisers from Clinton's entourage had been engaged). The texture of Brazilian society, marked by centuries of domestic slavery, continues to be a curious mixture of the deeply hierarchical and remarkably informal, a distinctive combination that produces a relaxed—not tense—kind of deference. Fernando Henrique's intellectual qualifications, outstanding by any measure, signified for this popular sensibility an ability to rule that Lula—his smallest grammatical error picked up by reporters—visibly lacked.

The contrast was compounded by the message of each candidate. Lula centred his campaign on the social sores that make

---

3   For the transcript of the exchange between the journalist Carlos Monforte and the minister Rubens Ricupero, see *Folha de S. Paulo*, 3 September 1994.

Brazil the most unequal industrial society in the world, trying to awaken voters to anger at the unbearable injustices around them. But often people don't want to be reminded too much of their own misery. Victor Kiernan once wisely remarked that if class consciousness has historically always been weaker among the exploited than the exploiters, one reason is simply that it is too discouraging to live with the constant thought of one's own ill fortune—some kind of escapism is virtually an existential necessity; whereas there is every satisfaction in frequent contemplation of wealth and power, if one possesses them. For many, Lula's indictments—however truthful—were dispiriting. Fernando Henrique, on the other hand, while not denying inequality or suffering, focussed his campaign on the vast potential of Brazil as a nation, and the bright future of its people, if the right kind of growth could again be achieved. Reforms were necessary too. But the key-note was hope, not indignation.

With this appeal, Fernando Henrique won the presidency by a landslide on the first ballot, with over twice the vote for Lula. Few electoral victories have been so decisive. The triumph had nevertheless a shadow. The political front that rallied behind Cardoso was wider than that previously behind Collor, for it included virtually every social force that had backed Collor, plus all the centre-left opinion that had rejected him. Yet, although the size of the electorate had increased and voting is compulsory, Fernando Henrique polled a total vote—34 million—slightly below that of Collor. Defying the law, 16 million abstained, and another 14 million cast blank or spoiled ballots—three times as many as in 1989. When counting was complete, it became clear that the electorate had in fact divided into three constituencies: those who voted for Fernando Henrique (36 per cent), those with no clear preference (33 per cent), and those who voted for other candidates (31 per cent). Disillusion with a decade of aimless democracy, and apathy at a contest with a too predictable outcome, set limits to the base of the new presidency. Cardoso will be inaugurated in January. The immediate priority of the incoming regime will be to prevent the *real* going the way of its predecessors. Fernando Henrique cannot afford any re-run of the cycle of Sarney or Collor. Inflationary pressures were tactically contained by both government and business to help elect his campaign—the head of the Employs Federation in São Paulo openly urging firms not to raise prices before polling-day. The exchange rate is overvalued, hitting exporters, and consumer credit has been tightened. To maintain stabilization, further austerity will be needed. But any sharply deflationary course would not only make confrontation with the trade-unions inevitable, but the keeping of campaign promises impossible. The centre-piece of Cardoso's programme was a pledge to invest $100 billion in infrastructural projects, to boost growth and generate employment, without raising taxes. A major inflow of foreign capital and sale of state enterprises are designed to cover the funding gap. Reforms of health, education, agriculture, housing and pensions are also promised—however, typically without spending targets. The constraints on them could be tight. Brazil is a federal union, in which the budget of the central state is currently so waterlogged by debt repayment and statutory obligations that only a quarter of total expenditure is discretionary. The fiscal system is notoriously chaotic and regressive —only 7 million out of an economically active population of 50 million pay income tax. Fernando Henrique is pledged to render it more equitable, without increasing total receipts (far below OECD levels, at about 25 per cent of GNP). But here he has remained studiously vague: tax reform is all too likely to split the coalition that elected him. His campaign literature says he will avoid 'simplistic solutions'. Squaring the different requirements of this prospectus is going to be a hard task. But the general direction of Cardoso's strategy is clear enough. It corresponds fairly closely, in fact, to the recommendations of Latin America's leading advocate of a post-socialist Left, Jorge Castañeda, in his recent major work *Unarmed Utopia*. The scenario runs roughly as follows. Sound money and moderate deregulation, restoring business confidence, will set the stage for stable growth and higher employment; while sale of state assets will create a compensation fund for social investment and reform. In practice, the scale of privatization is likely to be greater than currently admitted— nearer $50 than $15 billion may be needed to cover revenue shortfalls. The employment effect of spending programmes, on the other hand, is likely to be less than envisaged. The phenomenon of jobless growth is not confined to the developed countries: it has for some time been a marked feature of the Brazilian economy. Unemployment, after steadily rising over the past decade, now stands at an official (that is, understated) figure of 12 per cent. Cardoso, an admirer of Felipe González, has learnt the danger of too over-definite promises from the Spanish experience, and been careful to avoid any specific target of job creation. But the social thrust of his administration cannot be an optional extra: he will be vulnerable if there is no substantial improvement here. In the countryside, a modest goal of settling 280,000 landless families on uncultivated soil has been set. But given the nature of his agrarian allies, even this is not guaranteed. There is no magic way of reconciling the interests of capital and labour, landowners and peasants, middle and under-classes, in a society as staggeringly polarized as Brazil. Price stability, rapid growth, and income redistribution are a triad that has rarely been achieved by any government anywhere.

Still, against the scale of the social problems facing the new administration must be set its political assets. Since re-democratization, the Brazilian presidency has looked a weak institution. The Constitution of 1988 gave greater powers to Congress, and reduced the Union's share of public revenues —changes that certainly restrict the leeway of the federal executive. But the impression of debility owes much more to the incumbents than to the office. Sarney was not elected at the polls, Collor had no party behind him, and Itamar was a substitute. Their performances have obscured the reality that the presidency is a far more powerful authority in Brazil—juridically and politically—than in the United States. For it both controls an extensive public sector—the six largest firms in the country are all state enterprises—that gives it a steering capacity over the economy unknown to the White House, and confronts no organized counterweight in Congress, where partisan discipline is minimal compared even to the very low standards in the US legislature.

Brazil has always had the least significant party system of any country in South America, and the new Constitution has disintegrated it still further. The result is a fragmentation and confusion in Congress that can frustrate a weak president, incapable of dominating it, but offers fewer barriers to a strong president—or even just a freshly-elected one. Fernando Henrique knows the meanderings of the legislature, as an expert navigator, from within. He now arrives to head the executive, armed with a landslide mandate, great force of personality, and broad congressional support. There will not be many obstacles to his will in the first year.

There is an irony here. Historically, the presidency in Latin America is an import from the United States, imitated from the Constitution of 1783. A case could be made that it has done more damage south of the Rio Grande than Coca-Cola or the Marines. In recent years, for the first time since the days of Batlle in Uruguay, there has been growing criticism of it by Latin Americans as an invitation to autocracy and demagogy, and impediment to any responsible political system of parties and principles. This feeling was strong enough in Brazil to put the question of the best form of government, after much public discussion, to a referendum in 1993. In that debate Fernando Henrique and the PSDB rightly underlined the costs and dangers of presidentialism, and urged the adoption of a parliamentary system along European lines to strengthen democracy in Brazil. The PT, by contrast, having earlier championed parliamentarism, jettisoned that commitment—convinced it had a presidential winner in Lula—and backed the traditional system. It has now earned the reward for this opportunism. Fernando Henrique, on the other hand, after principled criticism of an over-mighty institution, has entered into possession of it. It seems likely the result will not be to diminish its powers, but to expand them. There is already talk of revising the Constitution to permit a second term, before the first has even started. Whatever else Cardoso might lack for a successful presidency, it will not be executive influence.

If 'political capacity', in Gramsci's phrase, marks the new ruler off from his predecessors, there is a further contrast that could be of even greater consequence. The platform on which Fernando Henrique has been elected is a moderate one. His campaign biography goes out of its way to declare: *Não é radical.* 'He is no radical'. It is possible—perhaps probable—that his practice will be yet more limited than his promises. Even in that event, however, he could still win the loyalty of the dispossessed.

For Brazil has suffered from an unbroken series of brutal or footling rulers for three decades now, not one of them—save the final off-beat locum—possessed of the smallest sensibility for the poor or down-trodden. At its height, the military regime ruled firmly and skilfully. But it was never liked: its most prosperous years, under Médici, were the period of greatest fear. The civilians who succeeded the generals proved to be liars and crooks, without even claims to competence. Against this dismal background, any half-way decent democrat is bound to shine. It is a long time since the Brazilian people—a sentimental nation—felt any affection for a president. A few gestures of real concern will now go a long way. The condition of millions remains so desperate that even a modicum of popular measures could create lasting gratitude. Critics of Fernando Henrique on the Left delude themselves if they imagine he will neglect these. Compassion and calculation alike make it certain he will not.

At the same time, the reactionary allies who ensured his victory cannot be ignored either. There is an illustrious precedent for the kind of balancing-act Fernando Henrique must now embark on. The long ascendancy of Getúlio Vargas in Brazilian politics (1930–54) was based on a dual system of support: traditional *coronelismo* in the countryside, and industrial populism in the cities, embodied in the two unequal parties he created after the war, the PSD of landowning elites and the PTB of paternalist unions. Today, the relative weight of rural and urban societies has altered completely; and the mechanisms of political control are no longer the same. Intimidation in the backlands has dwindled, and corruption of labour virtually disappeared. Face-to-face networks of patronage and dependency have lost ground to the powers of advertising and television. But a double schema of hegemony continues to be possible. Fernando Henrique's coalition of the PFL and PSDB—one party dominant in the North-East, the other emergent in the Centre-South—bears an evident resemblance to Getúlio's formula. His electoral front even included, on a nice antiquarian note, the rump of the PTB. This is an analogy that will only go so far. The paternalism of the Vargas era, and its epilogue under Kubitschek (1956–61), has passed. So too has their kind of nationalism: Cardoso will dismantle many of the state enterprises they built. 'Brazil is no longer an underdeveloped country', reads the first sentence of his manifesto. The claim is too simplified, but it is certainly true that Brazil now contains a modern society whose dynamics are structurally dominant in the country as a whole. In this sense, a more appropriate parallel for Fernando Henrique's administration might be Roosevelt's regime in the thirties. FDR too enjoyed the support of the most regressive oligarchy in the country, the Bourbon Democrats of the South—critical for his overall system of rule, but contained as a regional enclave within a political order otherwise resting on the loyalty of the urban masses. Cardoso has often expressed his admiration for the New Deal, and the atmosphere of his presidency—surrounded with reforming advisers of every kind—might come to recall it. The model of Roosevelt, of course, delineates a maximum of historical success and power.

There is one principal obstacle to such a prospect. Roosevelt had to face no significant force to his left. In American politics, a respectful Communist Party or an awkward John L. Lewis were marginalia. In Brazil, on the other hand, the PT is a central presence on the national stage. It is often described—even by its enemies—as the only real political party, with a genuine mass membership, in the country. There is an element of myth in this. The PT claims over half a million 'affiliates', but its actual members number only about 70,000. Unquestionably, however, their commitment and discipline are superior to those of any other party, many of which are mere labels for hire. Behind these militants stand a multitude of voters—last month some 17 million people preferred Lula to Cardoso. The party is less popular than this, with about 12 per cent of the vote for Congress. But the PT's ultimate strength lies in its roots in the unions. The party was born as a vehicle of organized labour, at a time when independent trade-unions were still few and weak. Today, the CUT—the confederation close to it—embraces 2,000 unions with 16 million members. Recent growth has been concentrated in the countryside, where rural unions are often important symbols, but lack striking power. In the towns, however, CUT unions are a formidable force—organizing everything from the federal police to banking, oil wells to auto plants, docks to hospitals—across public and private sectors, industry and services.

What kind of role is this labour movement likely to play under the new government? In Argentina, Peronist trade-union federations that were in the past much more powerful than any-thing in Brazil have been crushed with ease by Menem—who also has had no difficulty in co-opting the main opposition party, the Radicals, into a reform of the constitution to permit his own re-election. The comprehensive triumph of Argentine neo-liberalism, under a ruler of Peronist credentials, raises the question: could the same evolution occur, *mutatis mutandis*, in Brazil—where the stabilization programme already owes much to its example? There is a moral chasm between Cardoso and Menem as personalities. But the logic of their politics might still converge, when Fernando Henrique confronts—as he is

bound to do—resistance from the trade-unions. The outcome
is unlikely to be the same, however. Brazilian labour may have
less experience and tradition than its Argentinian counterpart,
but it has not been demoralized by thirty-five years of economic
stagnation and regression, and it is independent of the president.
A clean sweep of it is improbable. But division and confusion
are quite possible. In Congress, Fernando Henrique will have
many opportunities to play off Right against Left—relying on
the support of the PFL for neo-liberal measures, and appealing
to the good-will of the PT for social reforms. Moderates in the
PT—including many of its best talents—have always been close
to progressives in the PSDB. In due course Cardoso, lacking any
base of his own in organized labour, will perhaps try to split the
party and integrate this wing into his coalition. If he were to
pull this off, he would really have updated the Getulist formula.

It is too soon to say what the chances of such an operation
are. Ideologically, the PT is not a particularly united or coherent formation. It contains various potential lines of fissure. But
it is a democratic party, with a hard-won sense of the value of
grass-roots organization and genuine debate, and a collective
pride in its autonomy. The next years will be the real test of it.
Brazil is the only country in the world to have produced a new
working-class party of classical dimensions since the War. The
emergence of the PT not only defied a global trend, the decline
of labour politics throughout the capitalist world in the eighties,
but also a national pattern: the long-standing inexistence of any
serious parties in the largest Latin country.

Today it is widely believed that the epoch of mass party
systems as such is coming to an end. If this were so, Brazil—
having missed its moment—would now never know it, but
rather already anticipate the electronic politics of the future.

The PT would then be a quirk out of time, soon to pass. This is not an idle fancy. The fate of Solidarity, with which it was so often twinned, is a warning of what might occur. But everything is still in play. The most promising ruler and most challenging opposition of the nineties have yet to do battle. It is safe to say that Fernando Henrique will be the best president Brazil has ever had. But what kind of compliment—bearing predecessors in mind—that turns out to be, will depend on his adversaries more than his allies.

2

FERNANDO HENRIQUE

2002

For two decades—more or less since the Falklands War, and the end of the military dictatorships that had become an international byword for counter-revolutionary ferocity—South America has been largely forgotten by world politics. Recycled democratization, debt and dependency offered few conflicts and yielded no consequences to compare with dramas in Eastern Europe or Russia, the Middle or Far East, even domestic convulsions in North America itself. The days of the Cuban missile crisis might have belonged to another century. Today, there are once again tremors in this legendary margin of the larger arena. At one end of the continent, Argentina has seen a social breakdown that is neo-liberalism's version of the collapse of communism in the Soviet Union, amid the largest sovereign default in history. At the other, Venezucla teeters day by day on the brink of civil war. Till yesterday, these were the two richest societies of the region. In between, American gunships swarm over Colombia as guerrillas shell the Presidential Palace; exasperated Indian populations loft a radical colonel to power in Ecuador, where the dollar—thousands of miles from Washington—is now the official currency, and have come close to electing one of their own, a militant grower of coca (the other currency of the area), to the presidency in Bolivia. Under weak rulers, Peru and Paraguay are seething with discontent. Everywhere, economic crisis is biting hard.

In this landscape, the sweeping electoral victory in Brazil of a burly former metal-worker, from a family of twenty-two in the backlands, missing a little finger in an industrial accident, ungrammatical in speech and untutored in government, is the loudest rumble of thunder to date. With a population now approaching 180 million, more than the rest of the continent combined, Brazil towers over its neighbours, but has never historically led them. Whether this might change under Lula is one of the many uncertainties his capture of the presidency raises. Within the country itself, the nature of his triumph poses other enigmas. What kind of verdict does it represent, in the first instance, on the tenure of Fernando Henrique Cardoso, whose eight years in office end next January? Lula campaigned strongly against his record, and even the candidate of his own party avoided overly compromising mention of him. Yet opinion polls suggest Cardoso's standing as an individual has held up well, and there is no doubt that many Brazilians—principally, but not exclusively, from the middle classes—believe that he has been their most enlightened ruler to date.

Defenders of the outgoing president can point to a series of achievements, which—albeit exaggerated in official apologias— are real enough. Hyper-inflation was broken at the beginning of his rule, unambiguously benefiting the worst-off layers of the population. Illiteracy was reduced; infant mortality fell; there was some redistribution of land. If none of these advances was very spectacular—Brazil lags far behind even Mexico on the first and third, not to speak of Argentina or Chile on the second—the social ledger is not entirely bare. Nor, for that matter, is the administrative. The state apparatus has in certain respects undergone a genuine modernization, making it less opaque and more efficient. Levels of corruption, though still high, have fallen. Statistical information is somewhat more reliable, budgetary controls are tighter, regional pork-barrels are fewer. These are processes that have eroded the archaic oligarchies of the North-East, forces that helped Cardoso to power, but have been weakened under him: perhaps the most important long-run change of the period.

But if it is a mistake to dismiss such gains, they remain modest compared with the scale of the damage inflicted by the government's macro-economic policies. The defining character of the Cardoso presidency has been a neo-liberalism 'lite', as Brazilians—pioneers of nicotine images of politics—would say. In other words, the kind that predominated throughout the developed capitalist world in the nineties, when doctrines of the Third Way and the New Centre—Clinton, Blair, Schroeder—ostensibly distanced themselves from the harder versions of neo-liberalism pioneered by Reagan and Thatcher in the eighties, while in practice continuing, indeed often accentuating, the original programme, but now accompanied by secondary social concessions and a more emollient rhetoric. Throughout this period the fundamental dynamic of neo-liberalism has persisted, unabated: its two core principles— deregulation of markets and privatization of services (or industries, where still public)—setting the parameters of economic correctness. In the

United States, the brackish aftertaste of Clinton's White House made a sufficient number of voters too queasy to return Gore, but the real legacy of his rule was the striking down of Glass-Steagall, and the Bubble Economy that burst in the wake of his exit: Enron, Tyco and WorldCom were its parting signatures. In underdeveloped conditions, the sequence was necessarily different. Convinced that Brazil could not finance growth from domestic savings, and that its public enterprises fostered inefficiency and corruption, Cardoso overvalued the currency, put the state sector on the auction block and threw the economy open—gambling on imports to hold down inflation, and foreign investment to modernize infrastructure and industry. Brazil is a huge country, with a large internal market and abundant resources. Overseas capital duly flowed in—$150 billion by the end of his mandate. But it did little or nothing to dynamize the Brazilian economy, whose rates of investment remained sickly throughout Cardoso's rule. Attracted mainly by cheap assets and sky-high interest rates, foreign operators snapped up public enterprises, acquired local firms and—above all—bought state bonds. Trade deficits soared, interest rates were raised even further to prop up the currency, and debt levels became hopelessly vulnerable to loss of confidence, triggering enormous outflows whenever there was turbulence in international financial markets—Mexico in 1995, East Asia in 1997, Russia in 1998, Argentina in 2001—and an inevitable collapse of the exchange rate. Repeated IMF bail-outs merely deepened the pit of debt into which the country was being driven. When Cardoso came to power, the trade balance was in surplus, and public debt some 28 per cent of GDP; by the end of this year, it had doubled to 56 per cent, most of it held on short-term maturities. Under his presidency, per capita growth rate has been a miserable one per cent a year. The results of the Brazilian variant of neo-liberalism are plain for all to see: deepening stagnation, falling real wages, unprecedented unemployment, and a staggering debt burden. The regime stands condemned on its own terms. The government's original achievement—monetary stabilization—is in ruins: the currency is worth a quarter of its value at the outset of the Plano Real, interest rates are highest in the world, and the country is staring a moratorium in the face. Violent crime haunts the big cities as never before. Inequality remains virtually the worst anywhere. Dependency—in every deleterious sense—is incomparably deeper than it was when Cardoso, in his now distant past as a sociologist, once proposed a critical theory of it.

The logic of a neo-liberal model in the periphery of world capitalism puts any country that adopts it at the mercy of unpredictable movements in the financial markets of the centre, so Cardoso's misadventures were in large measure the chronicle of a fiasco foretold. But this was also a timorous and incompetent regime. The exchange rate was unsustainable from the start, overvalued for demagogic effect, and no thought was given even to the modest degree of capital controls that a dependent neo-liberalism still allows, which protected the Chilean economy from the ravages that Brazil was to suffer. More generally, of course, the whole notion that the key to successful attraction of foreign capital was deregulation and privatization à l'outrance was naive and provincial. In the same years that Cardoso was leading Brazil into its present blind alley, China was attracting foreign investment on a scale that dwarfed the hot money in Brazil, while maintaining tight capital controls and a non-convertible currency, to achieve the highest rates of GNP growth in the world. There is no shortage of acute problems, not to speak of inequalities and injustices, in China today. But the contrast between vigorous development and crippled dependency could not be starker.

Why did Fernando Henrique cling to a plainly calamitous path so long, when its logic was already clear in the first exchange-rate crisis in the spring of 1995? One explanation would point to the political pact with the old order—the landowners of the North-East, the bankers and media magnates of São Paulo and Rio—that brought him to power. The maxim of his strategy to win the presidency was *pas d'ennemis à droite*. Today, though he himself continues to speak otherwise, his admirers abroad—as any issue of *The Economist* reveals—do not hesitate to describe Cardoso's rule as a Centre-Right regime. In this interpretation, a distinguished statesman and intellectual of the Left became a captive of conservative alliances from which he could never free himself. Such a view, however, misconstrues the traditional oligarchies of the country, which have never been doctrinally inflexible—their instincts are utterly pragmatic or 'physiological', as the Brazilians put it—and often stood to lose from too strong doses of deregulation. A better answer probably lies in Cardoso's relationship to his finance minister, Pedro Malan, and through him to the IMF and the US in a wider sense.

The psychological dependence of a ruler on a technician, in the decisive area of contemporary government, has become an increasingly common pattern in this period. Next door, the relationship between Carlos Menem and Domingo Cavallo offered an even more striking example. The two pairs, Brazilian and Argentinian, were very different as human beings. Cavallo had a demonic side—also in his boldness and energy—that Malan, a quiet mediocrity, entirely lacks. Menem, completely ignorant of economics, allowed Cavallo to install the ultimate folly of a currency board, guaranteeing parity of the peso to the dollar.

But he had reason to fear him as a potential rival, and in due course they parted company. Cardoso, on the other hand, would probably have liked Malan to succeed him. Infinitely better prepared than Menem, he still remained by formation a sociologist, whose sense of disciplines no doubt inclined him to defer to a professional economist. The original stabilization of 1994 was the work of Malan and his team, and Cardoso owed everything to it. That moral debt made it difficult for him to jettison Malan along with Gustavo Franco, the brash novice he had installed as head of the Central Bank, when politically speaking, he should, in his own interest, have done so. When the inflated exchange rate of the Plano Real finally buckled, Franco was dropped. But Malan stayed, and Brazil's *fuite en avant* into the tunnel of debt rattled on.

In Cardoso's inability to separate himself from his chamberlain, there was a further and ultimately more decisive factor. Malan, an intimate of the IMF, enjoyed American confidence. These were the years in which Stanley Fischer, acting as itinerant bagman for Rubin and Summers, would disburse stand-by credits and loans from the IMF in sovereign disregard of its statutes, according to the political value of incumbent regimes around the world to Washington. The two chief beneficiaries of his largesse were Russia and Brazil, countries large and strategic enough to warrant special favours for rulers in them congenial to US interests, no matter how deficient their economic performance. Yeltsin and Cardoso were both rescued from electoral difficulties by timely injections of cash, since Washington wished to keep them in power. In Moscow, the guarantor of these transactions was Anatoly Chubais. In Brasília it was Malan. So long as he remained in office, Cardoso could be sure of exceptional treatment by the Fund and the Treasury.

This was a tie that in any case went with the grain. For Fernando Henrique, the United States was now the central point of external reference, in every sense. Originally, his culture—he was after all a leading Marxist intellectual in the sixties—had been much more European than American, and as late as the eighties he toyed with self-comparisons to Spanish social-democracy. But in the years of exile and return, there was a significant change. It was US foundations that made possible the research centre he set up in 1969, on coming back to Brazil, and when he entered the political arena, he made no secret of his belief that what Brazil needed was an equivalent of the Democratic Party, the makings of which he saw in the broad oppositional front to the dictatorship of those years, the MDB. By the time he was president, a decade and a half later, the power of the United States in the world had increased enormously, victory in the Cold War creating global hegemony of a kind never seen before.

Ideologically, Fernando Henrique had adapted to this ascendancy well before he entered the Palácio do Planalto. Sporadic friction over lesser tariffs or patents aside, matter for commercial attachés, the result was a more or less complete alignment with Washington on all major international issues. In effect, Brazil had virtually no foreign policy worth speaking of. Historically, this was scarcely a novelty. The military regime of the sixties and seventies, which possessed some sense of geopolitics, and pursued a line in Africa at sharp variance with the United States, was in this respect an exception. Cardoso came to power promising that Brazil would play a role in the world commensurate with the size of its new-found democracy. But in office he could have been a ruler of Honduras, unable to summon up the courage for so much as a ceremonial visit to Havana, where even Aznar or Carter found their way. His contemporary Guido di Tella, Argentina's foreign minister under Menem, a scholar of no less charm and distinction, once publicly described his country's foreign policy with the terse words: 'We have carnal relations with the United States. The rest of the world doesn't count'. Cardoso was incapable of such Hispanic *tranchant*—Portuguese is a more edulcorating idiom—but his diplomatic practice was the same. The principal difference was in rhetorical pretension. Abroad, he will be remembered mainly for those fatuous gatherings in New York, Florence and Berlin, solemnly discussing the Third Way, at which Clinton and Blair conferred with companions and underlings, to mounting derision even among media well-disposed to them. The comical windbaggery of these occasions did more to discredit Cardoso than he can have imagined: for someone of his past, they were the intellectual equivalent of Gorbachev's advertising of pizzas on TV.

Within Brazil, of course, such matters have been of little moment. There, Cardoso continues to be widely respected for another side of his tenure. In the eyes of admirers, his greatest civilizing achievement has been the consolidation of Brazilian democracy. Courteous to opponents, constitutional in conduct, Fernando Henrique has presided—it is argued—over a nation that has become more mature in its politics, and stable in its attachment to values of liberty and civility. The peaceful transfer of power to Lula due to take place in January, after an election cleansed of calumny or violence, will set the seal on his most enduring legacy to the country. A normal democratic life has finally taken root in soil long poisoned by Brazil's inheritance of racial slavery, rural oligarchy, populist demagogy and—last but not least—military tyranny.

This now standard defence of the Cardoso years reveals more about Brazilian identity than about democracy. Empires tend to give peoples who have enjoyed them a markedly self-absorbed, provincial outlook: a fate Brazilians have no more been able to escape than Britons or Americans. For the fact—obvious enough in any comparative perspective—is that the local preservation of democracy is no particular merit of Fernando Henrique, since it was never seriously threatened after the generals withdrew from power, and far from being a remarkable national feat, is a regional banality. All the other Latin American societies—Argentina, Chile, Uruguay—that underwent military dictatorships in the sixties and seventies have achieved as much, under colourless, or conservative, or even corrupt and autocratic rulers. From Aylwin to Frei to Lagos, from Sanguinetti to Lacalle to Batlle—no big deal. Even Menem, for whom it would be difficult to imagine a less democratic temperament, handed over power to de la Rua just as routinely as Cardoso will do to Lula in January.

Many Brazilians still find it difficult to remember their neighbours. Reminded of such common experiences, however, loyalists will concede that formally speaking, constitutional legality has been respected throughout the Southern Cone, and in that sense Cardoso's rule may seem nothing special. But substantively, the quality of Brazilian democracy—so the reply goes—has vastly improved during his presidency. Compared with the chaotic, turbulent years under Sarney, Collor and Itamar, his government has been a model of rational conduct and orderly dialogue, accustoming Brazilians to new norms of political decency and reliability, from which all interlocutors have benefited. Within a decade this is a striking accomplishment, which has done a great deal to civilize Brazilian society.

How is this claim to be judged? There is no doubt that Brazilian politics became calmer and more predictable under Cardoso, nor that the conventions of the New Republic, whose charter dates from 1988, became steadily more anchored in custom and habit. To that extent, it could even be said that not monetary but political stabilization was the real trademark of the presidency, the second plainly outlasting the downfall of the first. On the other hand, a glance at the statistics or stories of steadily escalating crime in the press is enough to indicate the limits of the new civility. While urbanities are swapped in the cupulas of power, violence rages as never before on the beaches and streets. A week before the second round of the presidential polls this October, the *Jornal do Brasil* bannered its Monday edition: 'Shootouts in Restaurant, Bus, School—8 Dead. A Normal Day in Rio'. In a single morning, sub-machine guns were blasting at the corner of the Avenida Atlantica in tourist Copacabana, in petty-bourgeois Niteroi across the bay and in the slums of the Zona Norte. Anglo-American viewers will soon be able to get a sense of such nightmares, with the release of the movie *City of God*, based on Paulo Lins's novel. They are unlikely to think the country is being civilized.

But it is not just the contrast between elite arrangements and popular misery that makes talk of a transformation of Brazilian political mores seem one-sided. Something more ideologically pointed is also at stake. For when people speak of the civilizing effect of Cardoso's government, what they are often actually referring to was its ability to tamp down the conflictual potential of Brazilian democracy, by setting the parameters of a consensus in which all serious dissent is disqualified in advance as outlandish and anachronistic: the local version of *la pensée unique*. Naturally, within this conformist corral, in which neo-liberal platitudes are taken as read, exchanges are well-mannered. But if we look at the institutional structures of power, a different picture emerges.

In Brazil, parties are often little more than labels of pecuniary convenience, alliances for dubious ends between the most incongruous partners a matter of course, and deputies transfer allegiances as frequently as football players. Before, and even for a short while after, he became president, Fernando Henrique spoke of the urgent need for political reform, to render the party system more principled and coherent as the first condition of improving democratic life in Brazil. At the end of eight years, what is the balance-sheet? There has been no change of any kind. In practice, Cardoso preferred to maintain the existing amorphous promiscuity, since it afforded such scope for his own outstanding skills in corridor negotiation and congressional manoeuvre. The 'reform' he forced through instead was the exact opposite: changing the Constitution to permit his own re-election as president. Politically speaking, this was certainly the worst single act of his rule, which will have the longest effects. It places him alongside Fujimori and Menem, whose example he imitated, as so many self-important egoists who degraded the legal traditions and democratic prospects of their countries. Latin America has always suffered from the bane of over-powerful presidentialism—historically, the worst single import from the United States, aggravated by the lack of Northern checks and balances, and seedbed of every kind of demagogy and autocracy. But at least the liberal oligarchs of the nineteenth century, and their successors in the twentieth, typically saw the sense of single-term limits. In Brazil, even the military dictatorship of the sixties and seventies did not tamper with this rule, showing sufficient collective self-discipline to pass the baton from one officer to another every five years.

There was no compelling reason, other than vainglory, for Cardoso to insist on re-election. Malan or Serra, his minister of health, could perfectly well have continued his regime in 1998, when they would have been elected without difficulty. In ramming through such a fundamental change, for such trivial motives, Fernando Henrique dealt a triple blow to Brazilian democracy. Firstly, by resorting to corruption to attain his ends—deputies from the depths of the Amazonian jungle were purchased to secure the necessary legislative majority—later waved away by their beneficiary with the immortal words: 'Someone may have sold their vote, the government didn't buy it.'[1] Secondly, by reinforcing the powers of an executive that already enjoys vast facilities of patronage and manipulation, and intensifying the personalization of politics, in the most deteriorated sense, around it. Finally, and perhaps most fatally, by the hypocrisy with which Cardoso orchestrated the campaign for his continuism—telling the nation, again and again, that he had nothing to do with the spontaneous desire that had arisen within Congress to permit a second term, a matter about which he was entirely neutral. Lying as brazen as this is an act of contempt, showing all too clearly the cynical realities behind the façade of an 'improved' Brazilian democracy.

If there was a single turning-point in Cardoso's rule, it was here. To see the political decay to which it has contributed, one only had to glance at the commercials with which every presidential candidate saw fit to deluge the nation this autumn. In the end, re-election rebounded against Fernando Henrique himself. If he had stepped down in 1998, his performance—though

---

1   A mantra repeated in various interviews after he left office: viz., 'FHC nega participar de suposto esquema de compra de votos para aprovar a reeleição', *Folha*, 12 June 2007.

its underlying logic was already plain enough—would have looked far better than it does in 2002. By clinging to power, he has ensured that he will be remembered for his economic myopia. In January 2003 he will exit in Mexican style—like López Portillo or Carlos Salinas, just able to defer the reckoning for his policies till he is out of office, but unlikely to be able to protect his reputation from what ensues. Unlike them, he never took financial advantage of his position. The treasury was not looted. But nor, unlike them, did he give the nation any passing period of growth either.

This is not to say that history will judge him a failure. It is too early for such a verdict, since his very economic mismanagement could paradoxically engender a long-term political success. For the legacy of debt he has left will lay such constraints on his successor that he has good reason to hope, as he proclaims, that his policies will live on after him, in the conduct of the new government. Nor is this the only way he has locked in those who will follow him. The ideological grip of the brand of conventional wisdom he came to represent remains, if not quite intact, still largely dominant in Brazil today, and with it the personalization of power he intensified. So, just as Thatcher can hail Blair as her most durable achievement—the transformation of the opposition into an updated version of her own rule—so Cardoso could still be able to congratulate himself that, after all, he had rendered a neo-liberal order in Brazil irreversible for some time to come.

On the face of it, Lula would seem an improbable candidate for the role that Fernando Henrique has so clearly cast him in. But Latin America abounds with examples of politicians or parties winning elections on platforms fiercely opposed to neo-liberalism, who once in power proceeded to implement neo-liberal policies, not infrequently more drastically than those they denounced for doing so in the first place. In Venezuela, Carlos Andrés Pérez was the first to follow this parabola, campaigning passionately against foreign debt and austerity, and then imposing an IMF-dictated package so savage it detonated the weeks of deadly rioting—the *Caracazo* of 1989—in a society then substantially richer per capita than Brazil today. In the same year, Fujimori beat Mario Vargas Llosa in Peru, denouncing the writer's repressive financial orthodoxy with a vehemence far exceeding any PT discourse today, and then became the architect of a particularly corrupt and cruel version of it. In Argentina, Menem's trajectory was essentially the same.

None of these figures situated themselves exactly on the Left, but in Europe we have seen the same cycle played out between Left and Right alike. France is the most eloquent case. Chirac came to power in 1995, denouncing *la pensée unique*—it was he who virtually patented the term—of the Mitterrand years. Once elected, his government promptly tried to impose classic neo-liberal reforms, which set off the great strikes of 1996, and lost him the elections of 1998, won by Jospin promising to do the opposite. Four years later, Jospin had privatized more than all previous governments put together, and the Socialist Party was in turn rejected at the polls this spring. Whatever the voters wanted in France, governments of either colour always did much the same. Time and again, promises were so much political confetti.

To note these precedents is not to say that Brazil is doomed to repeat the same cycle. Lula's capture of the presidency marks potentially a far deeper, and more hopeful, political change than any rotation of office in France. The symbolism of a former shoeshine-boy and street-vendor achieving supreme power in the most unequal major society on earth speaks for itself. Although other Brazilian presidents have been of comparatively humble origins, they all made their way to the top through further—military or civilian—education. Lula, a trade-union leader in his twenties, remains culturally a worker from a poor rural family, raised in the industrial belt round São Paulo, whose Portuguese is imperfect, and formal learning minimal. In private, with a nice touch of irony, he has remarked: 'Bush and I must be the two most ignorant presidents in the world'. Like his Northern counterpart, he has a streak of laziness, alongside a by now considerable acquired shrewdness. Across successive presidential campaigns, he has honed a macho charm capable of seducing middle-class audiences and disarming opponents, as well as electrifying popular masses. To see him at the microphone in the Canecão, a traditional music-hall in Botafogo, in the last days of the campaign, surrounded by composers, singers, actresses, writers—labour wooing culture—explaining to the crowd that he had been to Rio for political meetings many times, but could never wander barefoot on the sand of its beaches like any other citizen, was to watch a theatrical performance as professional as any in that setting.

All this can encourage myth-making. Brazilian culture is sentimental as well as cynical—the two, as one would expect, going together—and the local media are currently in biographical over-drive, as if social origins were a safe guide to political conduct. The example of Wałesa should be warning enough against excesses in this department. That said, it remains the case that Lula embodies a life-experience of popular hardship and a record of social struggle from below that no other ruler in the world approaches. His bond with the poor sets him apart. This is his primary constituency, and he will care how they rate him in power. Behind him, moreover, is the only new mass party to have been created out of the labour movement since the Second

World War—an organization that in numbers, influence, and relative cohesion has no equal in Latin America. The PT, which currently claims some 300,000 members, though criteria are not strict, is now, after administering a string of Brazil's largest cities—São Paulo, Belém, Recife, Brasília, Porto Alegre—a much more moderate organization than it was in the eighties. But it is still relatively free-form, without a fully centralized bureaucratic apparatus, and contains many militants who have not forgotten their radical past. Last but not least, there is the mass sentiment expressed in the presidential poll itself. The wretched of the Brazilian earth—those officially classified as 'poor and indigent' who make up nearly half the population—cast their votes for him in huge numbers. In the coastal cities of Rio and Salvador, with their black populations, Lula had landslide majorities: 79 and 89 per cent respectively. A climate of popular expectation surrounds Lula that no president of the New Republic has ever enjoyed at the outset of their mandate. Hope of relief from the misery of the last years will not vanish overnight.

On the other hand, against all such subjective build-up must be set the objective constraints of the situation in which president and party will now find themselves. First and foremost, of course, there is the landscape of economic wreckage left by Malan and Cardoso. Already before taking office, the PT leadership has strapped itself—in some cases, with well-nigh masochistic zest—into the Procrustean bed laid out by the IMF, a 'primary surplus' of 3.75 per cent of GDP, which will not only exclude any significant increase, but is likely to dictate a severe contraction of social spending, to win the confidence of foreign creditors and keep interest rates from climbing still higher.

At the same time, social mobilization remains depressed at levels far below those of the eighties—one of the effects of the

Cardoso years, weakening the collective energies always needed to confront emergencies. Here the very scale of Lula's victory at the polls is an ambiguous blessing. In the second round, he piled up 52 million votes, crushing Serra by 61 to 39 per cent. In part, this plebiscite was tribute to Lula's own tireless criss-crossing of the country, to its remotest corners, which no other candidate attempted.

But it was also the product of a saccharine public relations and propaganda campaign, orchestrated around the sickly watchword 'Lula—Peace and Love', and projected through television commercials of uninhibited effrontery, designed by a former key strategist of the business Right. Brazilian political advertisements are longer than American, allowing for more serious argument—but also for more flamboyantly manipulative kitsch. Lula's outclassed Serra's in every respect, not least the sums of money spent on them. Their signature gesture was the beckoning hand—of nubile nymphs, sports stars, average joes—inviting the viewer, to the rhythms of exuberant music, into bandwagon or bed, in the name of the motto. Once Lula had established a commanding lead in the opinion polls, the *Globo* empire—Brazil's Murdoch—started to smile on him, and money poured into his campaign coffers from banks and firms, making him paradoxically by far the best-financed of all the candidates. Such support is not given free.

Then too, powerful though the presidency is, legislation must pass Congress. There the PT has become for the first time the largest party, but in a fragmented spectrum in which it commands less than a fifth of seats in the assembly. Lula's national vote was double that of the party, which failed to gain the governorship of any important states. The imbalance between executive and legislative scores will be accentuated by the enhanced presidency, whose vast powers of patronage—some 20,000 posts are in its gift—anyway risk absorbing too many PT militants. For his electoral campaign, Lula adopted a paternalist textile millionaire, from a small Evangelical party, as his vice-presidential candidate, and picked up the endorsement of not a few disgruntled or opportunist oligarchs from the North-East. For a workable majority in Congress, he has already had to extend such alliances. The PT's political manager, José Dirceu—former exile in Cuba, underground operative for a decade on his return to Brazil—will be in control of this front. But it would be naive to imagine much radical legislation speeding out of the new Chamber.

Beyond these liabilities, there is also the weight of cultural tradition that will bear on the agents of any renovation. Far more even than Italy, which gave the concept to the world, Brazil is par excellence the land of *trasformismo*—the capacity of the established order to embrace and invert forces of change, until they become indistinguishable from what they set out to oppose. The career of Fernando Henrique, former Marxist become a pillar of the Centre-Right, has been a typical expression of this culture, of which he is both imprint and instrument. Lula's plebeian background is no bar to embrace by the establishment. Social hierarchy has always formed an easy connubium with affable informality in Brazil, and there is no reason to think that—without precautions—the backing of banks today could not become the neutering of an upstart tomorrow. The rhetorical conditions for such an outcome have already been prepared. Peace and love are, in advance, a vocabulary of ingestion and defeat. A cause can survive a slogan, but without better ones than this, objective pressures will crush subjective intentions soon enough.

But here, of course, programmes—as distinct from catchwords—become decisive. What does the incoming government propose to the country? Viewing its prospects statically, it would be difficult to avoid pessimism. In opposition, the PT has not been uncreative. The participatory budgets of Porto Alegre, where voters determine the distribution of spending in their wards, are an invention widely admired abroad. PT economists were the first to point out the logic of Malan's neo-liberalism, and predict its fatal consequences. But overall, it is obvious that neither party nor president have any articulated alternative to the reigning orthodoxy, as their pre-electoral adherence to the directives of the IMF made clear. On the other hand, historically, actual policy innovations in Latin America have seldom followed preconceived schemes. Out of the great crisis that shook the continent in 1929, arose a set of pragmatic, intuitive responses—essentially, different forms of import-substituting populism: Getulismo in Brazil, Peronism in Argentina, the MNR in Bolivia—that were creative and effective in their time. The ECLA doctrines formulated by Raúl Prebisch that were later associated with them crystallized *post facto*, more than guiding the actors in advance. South America today faces, once again, a crisis of continental proportions. Why should not Brazil, or its neighbours, once more find a way out of its impasse in similar fashion—with ingenious *ad hoc* solutions?

The difference, of course, lies in the immeasurably greater degree of integration of these economies, societies and cultures in the global order of capital, commanded from the North. The material and ideological intermeshing of national agents and processes with international structures that penetrate and mould them has no comparison with the situation in the Depression, when Latin America was left largely to its own devices once Wall Street had crashed. To that extent, the programmatic requirements for breaking out of the present straitjacket appear much higher. But if the central economies themselves should go into a tail-spin—were the United States to enter the trajectory of Japan in the last decade—then, as the empire attended to its homelands, the possibilities of improvised invention in the periphery might be released once more.

3

LULA

2011

Contrary to a well-known English dictum, stoical if self-exonerating, all political lives do not end in failure. In post-war Europe, it is enough to think of Adenauer or De Gasperi, or perhaps even more impressively, Franco. But it is true that, in democratic conditions, to be more popular at the close than at the outset of a prolonged period in office is rare. Rarer still—indeed, virtually unheard-of—is for such popularity to reflect, not an appeasement or moderation, but a radicalization in government. Today, there is only one ruler in the world who can claim this achievement: the former worker who in January stepped down as president of Brazil, enjoying the approval of 80 per cent of its citizens. By any criterion, Luiz Inacio da Silva is the most successful politician of his time.

That success has owed much to an exceptional set of personal gifts, a mixture of warm social sensibility and cool political calculation, or—as his successor Dilma Rousseff puts it—rational assessment and emotional intelligence, not to speak of lively good humour and personal charm. But it was also, in its origins, inseparable from a major social movement. Himself coming from the depths of the Brazilian poor, Lula's rise from worker on the shop-floor to leader of his country was never just an individual triumph: what made it possible was the most remarkable trade-union insurgency of the last third of a century, creating Brazil's first—and still only—modern political party, which became the vehicle of his ascent. Together, the combination of a charismatic personality and a nationwide mass organization were always formidable assets.

Nevertheless, Lula's success was far from a foregone conclusion. Elected in 2002, his administration got off to a dour start, and soon came close to disaster. His first year in office, dominated by the economic legacy of his predecessor, reversed virtually every hope on which the Workers' Party had been founded. Under Fernando Henrique Cardoso, the public debt—nearly half of it denominated in dollars—had doubled, the current account deficit was twice the Latin American average, nominal interest rates were over 20 per cent and the currency had lost half its value in the run-up to the election.[1] Argentina had just declared the largest sovereign default in history, and in the eyes of financial markets Brazil looked on the brink of the same precipice. To restore investor confidence, Lula installed an unblinkingly orthodox economic team at the Central Bank and Finance Ministry, which hiked interest rates yet further and cut public investment, to achieve a primary fiscal surplus higher than the figure the IMF itself had demanded. For citizens, prices and

---

1 Aline Diniz Amaral, Peter Kingstone and Jonathan Krieckhaus, 'The Limits of Economic Reform in Brazil', in Peter Kingstone and Timothy Power (eds), *Democratic Brazil Revisited*, Pittsburgh 2008, pp. 145–6.

unemployment rose as growth fell by a half. But what was bitter medicine for militants was nectar to bond-holders: the spectre of default was banished. Growth resumed in 2004, as exports recovered. But the public debt continued to rise, and interest rates were hoisted once more. Adherents of the previous regime, who had smarted under Lula's criticisms of Cardoso, pointed triumphantly to the continuities between the two. For the PT there was little to boast about.

If this was uninspiring enough, worse was to come. In the spring of 2005, the leader of one of the smaller parties in Congress (there were over a dozen of these), coming under pressure after one of his henchmen was videotaped pocketing a bribe, hit back with the revelation that the government had been systematically buying the votes of deputies, to the tune of $7,000 a month each, to secure majorities in the legislature. In charge of the operation was the head of Lula's cabinet in the Presidential Palace, José Dirceu, the money coming from illegal funds controlled by the PT and distributed by its treasurer Delúbio Soares. Within weeks of this bombshell, an aide to the brother of the chairman of the PT, José Genoino, was arrested boarding a flight with 200,000 *reais* in a suitcase and $100,000 dollars in his underpants. A month later, the manager of Lula's bid for the presidency, Duda Mendonça—a notoriety in the PR world—confessed that his campaign had been financed by slush funds extracted from interested banks and enterprises, in violation of electoral law, and that he himself had been rewarded for his services with secret deposits to an account in the Bahamas. Next it was the turn of one of Lula's closest political confidants, former trade-union leader Luiz Gushiken, under fire for siphoning pension funds for political ends, who was forced to step down as secretary of communications. In a yet darker background, lay the unresolved murder in early 2002 of Celso Daniel, mayor of the PT stronghold of Santo André, widely suspected of being a contract killing over bribes collected from local bus companies.[2] The exposure of a broad hinterland of corruption behind Lula's conquest of power, while it came as a demoralizing shock to much of the PT's own base, could be put—as it promptly was by loyalists—in historical perspective. Illegal bankrolling of campaigns by hidden donors in exchange for favours was widespread in Brazilian politics: the president of the main opposition party, Cardoso's PSDB, was caught on the same charge and had to resign amid the same scandal. Buying votes in Congress was no novelty. It was well known that Cardoso had greased the palms of deputies from Amazonas to secure the constitutional change that allowed him to run for a second term. The Brazilian legislature had long been a cesspit of venality and opportunism. By the end of Lula's first term, a third to two-fifths of the deputies in Congress had switched parties.[3] By the end of the second, over a quarter of both Houses were under criminal indictment or facing charges.[4] Currently, legislators are pressing for salaries of over $200,000 a year. In 2002, Lula had been elected with 61 per cent of the popular vote, but the PT got less than a fifth of the seats in Congress, where allies had to be found

---

2   There seems as yet to be no really good Brazilian study of the scandals of 2005–06, most treatments remaining partial and superficial. For a sober, if relatively brief, account in English, see Richard Bourne, *Lula of Brazil. The Story So Far*, London and New York 2008, pp. 176–95, which is also the most level-headed biographical study in any language of its subject to date.

3   For a lower estimate (31 per cent), see Fabiano Santos and Márco Grijó Vilarouca, 'Political Institutions and Governability from FHC to Lula', in Kingstone and Power (eds), *Democratic Brazil Revisited*, p. 77; for a higher (38 per cent)—195 out of 513 deputies—see the *Economist*, 14 April 2007.

4   *Economist*, 10 July 2010.

for the government to command a legislative majority. Dirceu had wanted to make a deal with the largest party of the centre, the PMDB, but this would have meant conceding it important ministries. Lula preferred to stitch together a patchwork of the smallest parties, whose bargaining power was weaker. But they naturally expected a lower-grade share of the spoils too, and so the *mensalão*—the monthly backhander—was devised for them.

In cash terms, the corruption from which the PT benefited, and over which it presided, was probably more systematic than that of any predecessor. In absolute terms, Brazilian elections are second only to American in their costs, and relative to national income can exceed them by a wide margin. In 1996, Clinton spent $43 million to take the White House; in 1994, Cardoso laid out $41 million to secure the Palácio do Planalto, in a country with a per capita GDP less than a sixth that of the United States.[5] Unlike Cardoso, who twice sailed to victory on the first ballot as the establishment candidate, and commanded abundant natural—in Brazilian parlance, 'physiological'—allies and placemen in Congress, Lula was a three-times loser when he ran again for the presidency in late 2002, and his party traditionally an object of the deepest suspicion to all who counted economically. To mount that unfavourable gradient, special resources were needed, for which special undertakings had to be given, public and private.[6] So too, with a smaller core of

5 See David Samuels, 'Money, Elections and Democracy in Brazil', *Latin American Politics and Society*, Summer 2001, 2, pp. 31–3. Cardoso outspent Lula by over 20:1 in 1994 and 18:1 in 1998. At the legislative level, in 1994 it cost an average $530,000 to elect a Congressman in the US, and $132,000 in Brazil—in American terms, the equivalent of around $800,000.

6 Some of the *caixa dois* money was probably also used for internal purposes, to ensure the dominance of the *Articulação* faction headed by Dirceu. For

deputies and fewer spontaneous friends in the legislature, to obtain makeshift majorities in Congress the PT was driven to bribe on a bigger scale.

Perhaps one could speak of a kind of workers' premium, in corruption as in disinflation—the need to over-satisfy the IMF with an excessive primary surplus to keep the economy on keel, the need to over-extract and distribute black money to win office and exercise power. That, at least, would have been one line open to the party's defenders. In practice, the more typical mitigation was to point to the personal probity, in some cases heroic record, of those in charge of disbursements made for organizational, not individual ends. Dirceu, the architect of the modern PT, and strategist of Lula's victory, had worked underground in the country for years after returning clandestinely from exile in Cuba. Genoino had been a guerrilla fighter in the jungle, imprisoned and tortured by the generals. Gushiken still lived the modest life of a former trade-unionist. They had acted without personal advantage, *pour les besoins de la cause*.

Such pleas did not move the media. Uniformly hostile to the PT anyway, the Brazilian press went into high gear as the scandal of the *mensalão* broke, sparing no deadly conjecture or damaging detail. Its target now lay wide open. There was no denying that the PT had always claimed to be a political force on a plane above the swamp of traditional mores, a fearless enemy of ingrained corruption rather than a hardened practitioner of it. Soon even the distinction between institutional misconduct and individual degeneration was swept away, in spectacular fashion. The single

---

this, see David Samuels, 'Brazil: Democracy under Lula and the PT', in Jorge Dominguez and Michael Shifter, *Constructing Democratic Governance in Latin America*, third edition, Baltimore 2008, p. 168.

most powerful figure in the government was the minister of
finance, Antonio Palocci, a mayor from the interior of São Paulo,
who had been the inspiration behind 'Letter to the Brazilians',
Lula's electoral billet-doux to the business community, and the
key broker for the PT's back-door transactions with banks and
construction firms during the campaign. A mediocre former
doctor, with no particular economic skills, his *sub rosa* ties to
assorted cash-boxes and rigid orthodoxy in office made him the
guarantee of business confidence in the government and toast
of the financial press, at home and abroad. Shady deals in his
municipal fief of Riberão Preto had long been rumoured, though
these too could be minimized as replenishing only coffers of
the party.

But in early 2006, it emerged that a secluded lakeside
mansion in Brasília had been rented by one of his aides from
Riberão Preto. There, in scenes out of Buñuel, the sallow features of the finance minister—he looks like a cut-purse in some
low-life *seicento* painting—were to be glimpsed slipping from
limousine to portal, to enter a villa where rooms were equipped
only with beds, and a side-table or two for cash and alcohol. Here
discreetly came and went lobbyists and familiars, along with the
minister, to enjoy prostitutes and parties, and exchange tips and
favours. When the news of this brothel came out, cynics could be
heard to say that there was no reason for surprise, the capital itself
being little more than an enlarged version of the same. Palocci,
who was not in a position to take this line, made desperate
attempts to stifle the affair. Lula too, comparing him effusively
to Ronaldinho as 'the star player whom the team cannot afford
to lose',[7] sought by every means to save him, in vain. With his fall

---

7 *Veja*, 24 November 2005.

in the spring of 2006, the slate of the leading politicians around the presidency was virtually wiped clean.

The uproar over these scandals in the media was deafening. In Congress the opposition pressed for one commission of investigation after another. Leading members of the PSDB started to talk of impeaching Lula himself for complicity in the corruption of his entourage. Feeling cornered by this wave of assaults, which he compared with the attacks that had led to the suicide of Getúlio Vargas in the Presidential Palace in 1954, Lula began to speak in private of appealing to the streets if his enemies persisted in trying to depose him. In reality, there was little danger of this, since both Cardoso and Serra—the PSDB mayor of São Paulo beaten by Lula in 2002, but hoping to become the presidential candidate again for his party later that year—decided it would be better to leave a badly wounded incumbent in office than to risk the emergence of a strong uncompromised opponent if he were ousted.

Rarely has a political calculation so misfired. Besieged in the media and mauled in the legislature, Lula could rely on two reserves that not only saved his position, but transformed it. The first was the return of sustained economic improvement. After a period that had seen the worst stagnation of the century—an annual average growth of 1.6 per cent in the nineties, creeping up to no more than 2.3 per cent in Cardoso's eight years—GDP increased at a clip of 4.3 per cent from 2004 through 2006. The jump was essentially due to external good fortune. These were the years in which Chinese demand for Brazil's two most valuable exports, soya and iron ore, took off, amid a steep general rise in commodity prices. In America, where interest rates were being held artificially low by the Fed to keep the financial bubble in the United States from bursting, the 'Greenspan put' made a flow of cheap capital imports available to Brazil. As business and jobs picked up, the mood in the country changed. Few voters were disposed to quibble with official claims of credit for the improvement. With the upturn, moreover, the state was now collecting larger revenues. These would be critical for the government's other ace.

From the start, Lula had been committed to helping the poor from whom he came. Accommodation of the rich and powerful would be necessary, but misery had to be tackled more seriously than in the past. His first attempt to do so, a 'Zero Hunger' scheme to assure minimum sustenance to every Brazilian, was a mismanaged fiasco. In his second year, however, consolidating various pre-existent partial schemes and expanding their coverage, he launched the programme that is now indelibly associated with him, the *Bolsa Família*—a monthly cash transfer to mothers in the lowest income strata, against proof that they are sending their children to school, and getting their health checked. The payments are very small—currently $12 per child, or an average $35 a month. But they are made directly by the federal government, cutting out local malversation, and now reach over 12 million households, a quarter of the population. The effective cost of the programme is a trifle.[8] But its political impact has been huge. This is not only because it has helped, however modestly, to reduce poverty and stimulate demand in the worst-afflicted regions of the country. No less important has been the symbolic message it delivers—that the state cares for the lot of every Brazilian, no matter how wretched or

---

8   Marcelo Neri, 'Income Policies, Income Distribution, and the Distribution of Opportunities in Brazil', in Lael Brainard and Leonardo Martinez Diaz (eds) *Brazil as an Economic Superpower?: Understanding Brazil's Role in the Global Economy*, Washington DC, 2009, p. 242; *Economist*, 31 July 20, 2010.

down-trodden, as citizens with social rights in their country. Popular identification of Lula with this initiative became his most unshakeable political asset. Materially, a succession of substantial increases in the minimum wage was to be of much greater significance. These began just as the corruption scandals were breaking. In 2005, a rise in real terms double that of the previous year was decreed. In the election year of 2006, the rise was greater still.[9] By 2010, the cumulative increase in the rate was 50 per cent. Still under $300 a month, this remains well below the earnings of virtually any worker in formal employment. But since pensions are indexed to the minimum wage, its steady increase has benefited at least 18 million people directly—the Statute of the Elderly, passed under Lula, consolidating their gains.[10] Indirectly, too, it has encouraged workers in the informal sector not covered by the official rate, who make up the overwhelming majority—80 per cent—of the Brazilian work-force, to use the minimum as a benchmark to improve what they can get from their employers. Reinforcing these effects was the introduction of *crédito consignado* from early on—bank loans for household purchases to those who had never before had bank accounts, with repayment automatically deducted from monthly wages or pensions.[11] Together, conditional cash transfers, higher minimum wages and novel access to

---

9 R$ 240 in 2003, R$ 260 in 2004, R$ 300 in 2005, R$ 350 in 2006: Nelson Barbosa and José Antônio Pereira de Souza, 'A Inflexão do Governo Lula: Política Econômica, Crescimento e Distribuição de Renda' in Emir Sader and Marco Aurélio Garcia (eds), *Brasil entre o Passado e o Futuro*, São Paulo 2010, pp. 65, 75.

10 The Statute was passed early on, in late 2003.

11 From 2001 to 2006, consumer borrowing doubled as a proportion of GDP: Wendy Hunter and Timothy Power, 'Rewarding Lula: Executive Power, Social Policy, and the Brazilian Elections of 2006', *Latin American Politics and Society*, Spring 2007, p. 15.

credit set off not only a sustained rise in popular consumption, but also an expansion of the domestic market that finally, after a long drought, created more jobs.

In combination, faster economic growth and broader social transfers have accomplished the greatest reduction in poverty in Brazilian history. By some estimates, the number of the poor dropped from around 50 to 30 million in the space of six years, and the number of the destitute was halved.[12] Of this dramatic transformation half can be attributed to growth, half to social programmes—financed, of course, by higher revenues accruing from growth. Nor have such programmes been confined to income support. Since 2005 government spending on education has trebled, and the number of university students doubled. During the nineties, higher education in Brazil largely ceased to be a public function, three-quarters of all students going to private universities enjoying tax exemption. Astutely, these establishments have been obliged, in exchange for their exemption, to offer places to students from poor or non-white families who would otherwise never have a chance of getting beyond middle school, but can count on such scholarships to make it to college. However poor the quality of instruction—it is often terrible—the hope of betterment has made the programme, enrolling some 700,000 students to date, a great popular success, sometimes optimistically compared for democratizing effect to the GI Bill of Rights in post-war America.

In 2006, not all of this was yet achieved. But more than enough had been done to shield Lula from the battering of his adversaries. Popular opinion was not entirely indifferent to corruption—at the height of the *mensalão*, his ratings had

---

12 *Economist*, 3 July 2010: estimates of Marcelo Neri and Ricardo Paes de Barros, respectively of the Fundação Vargas and of IPEA.

dropped quite sharply. But measured against such appreciable improvements to life, back-handers did not count. By the spring, the political tables had been turned so completely that Serra, looking at the opinion polls, decided he had no chance against Lula, leaving a hapless rival in his party to be thrashed in the presidential election that autumn, when Lula walked away with the same majority as four years before—61 per cent in the second round. This time, however, its social composition differed. Alienated by the *mensalão*, much of the middle-class electorate that had rallied to Lula in 2002 deserted him, while the poor and the elderly voted for him in greater numbers than ever before.[13] His campaign, too, struck a different note. Four years earlier, when its aim had been to reassure doubtful voters, his managers had marketed him as the bearer of 'Love and Peace' to the country. In 2006 the tone was less saccharine. Brushing aside lapses in the PT of which he had, of course, been unaware, the president launched an aggressive counter-attack on the privatizations of the previous regime, which had enriched a few at the expense of the nation, and could be expected to resume if his opponent were elected. Far from any continuity, there was a gulf between his government and that of Cardoso: not a single enterprise had been privatized under it. The disposal of public assets, often on the murkiest terms, has never been popular in Brazil. The message struck home.

---

13 For the importance of the old in the electoral shift to Lula, see Simone Bohn, 'Social Policy and Vote in Brazil', *Latin American Research Review*, Vol. 46, No. 1, 2011, pp. 64–6. Much the largest single jump in his vote in 2006 came from those over sixty, where it doubled. To the material benefits which the elderly had gained since 2003 should no doubt be added the psychological factor that would be picked out by André Singer—fear of instability, for obvious reasons likely to be particularly marked among older people. If in 1989 the old were the age-group that lent least support to Lula, and by 2006 the most, the reassurance offered by his incumbency was no doubt a critical element in the shift.

Buoyed by socio-economic success and a more hard-hitting political victory, Lula's second mandate was a much more confident affair than the first. He was now not only the undisputed master of popular affection, as the first president to bring a modest well-being to so many of his people, but in complete control of his own administration. His two leading ministers were gone. Palocci—to Lula 'more than a brother'—he might regret personally, but was no longer required to calm the nerves of overseas investors. Dirceu, a virtuoso of cold political calculation and intrigue, he had never much liked and somewhat feared. Their joint elimination freed him for sole command in Brasília. When mid-way through his second term its test came, he handled it with aplomb. The crash of Wall Street in 2008 might be a tsunami in the US, he declared, but in Brazil it would be no more than a 'ripple'—*uma marolinha*. The phrase was seized on by the press as proof of economic ignorance and reckless irresponsibility.

But he was as good as his word. Counter-cyclical action was prompt and effective. Despite falling tax revenues, social transfers were increased, reserve requirements were reduced, public investment went up, and private consumption was supported. In overcoming the crisis, local banking practices helped.[14] Tight controls, holding multipliers of the monetary base well below US levels and greater transparency had left Brazilian banks in much better shape than those in US, protecting the country from the worst of the financial fall-out. But it was concerted, vigorous state policy that pulled the economy round. Lula's optimism was functional: told not to be afraid, Brazilians went out and consumed, and demand held up. By the second quarter of 2009, foreign capital was flowing back into the country, and by the end of the year the crisis was over. As Lula's second mandate came

---

14 For details, see Barbosa and Pereira de Souza, 'A Inflexão do Governo Lula', pp. 84–95.

to an end, the economy was posting over 7 per cent growth, and nature itself was smiling on his rule, with the discovery of huge deposits of offshore oil. To these domestic successes could be added foreign laurels. The international standing of Brazil has rarely, if ever, corresponded to its size or potential importance. Cardoso had consorted with the Clintons and Blairs of the North, but such company had only discredited him, as a lesser mouth-piece for the guff of the Third Way. Diplomatically, the guideline of his regime was fidelity to the United States. From the outset, Lula steered another course. Without confronting Washington, he gave greater priority to regional solidarity, promoting Mercosur with neighbours to the south, and refusing to cold-shoulder Cuba and Venezuela to the north. The most impressive figure in Lula's Cabinet, Foreign Minister Celso Amorim, was soon leading a front of poorer states to thwart Euro-American attempts to ram more 'free trade' arrangements—free for the US and EU—through the WTO at Cancún. As he politely expressed it: 'Cancún will be remembered as the conference that signalled the emergence of a less autocratic multilateral trading system'.[15] If Washington and Brussels have still not succeeded, eight years later, in imposing their will on the less developed world in the abortive Doha Round, credit must first of all go to Brazil.

In his second mandate, Lula would go much further in putting his country on the world stage. By now he was a statesman courted in every region of the world, who no longer had to defer, at least not outwardly, to the conventions of the 'international community'. In part this change was due to the increasing

---

15 'The Real Cancún', *Wall Street Journal*, 25 September 2003.

weight of Brazil as an economic power.[16] But it also reflected his own aura as the most popular ruler—in both senses of the term, political and social—of the age. Consecration of the new position he had won for his nation came with the formation of the BRIC quartet of powers in 2009, bringing the heads of state of Brazil, Russia, India and China together in one-time Sverdlovsk, with a communiqué calling for a global reserve currency. The following year Lula hosted the BRIC summit in Brazil itself. On paper, the four largest powers outside the Euro-American imperium would appear to represent, if not an alternative, at least some check to its dominion. Yet it is striking that, although it alone of the four is not a major military power, Brazil is so far the only one to have defied the will of the United States on issues of strategic importance to it—Lula not only recognizing Palestine as a state, but declining to fall in with the blockade of Iran, even inviting Ahmadinejad to Brasília. For Brazil to do this was a virtual diplomatic declaration of independence. Washington was furious, and the local press beside itself at this breach of Atlantic solidarity. Few voters cared. Under Lula, the nation had emerged as a global power. By the end, his vast popularity was a reflection not only of material betterment, but also of collective pride in the country.

If such is the bald record of this presidency, how is it to be interpreted historically? Three contrasting views hold the field in Brazil. For Cardoso and his followers, still dominant in much of the intelligentsia and all of the media, Lula embodies the most regressive traditions of the continent, his rule just another variant

---

16 In 2008, traditionally debt-ridden Brazil became for the first time a net foreign creditor, and by 2009 held foreign currency reserves of $250 billion, much of it in Treasury bills, making it the fourth-largest creditor of the United States. See Riordan Roett, *The New Brazil*, Washington DC, 2010, p. 116; Larry Rohter, *Brazil on the Rise*, New York 2010, p. 139.

of the demagogic populism of a charismatic leader, contemptuous at once of democracy and civility, purchasing the favour of the masses with charity and flattery. In Brazil this was the disastrous legacy of Vargas, a dictator who had returned to power through the ballot-box as 'father of the poor', and committed a melodramatic suicide when the criminality of his regime was exposed. In Argentina, the reign of Perón had been still more ruinous and corrupting. No less manipulative and authoritarian, if on a pettier scale, Lulismo is—Cardoso's verdict—'a kind of sub-Peronism'.[17] The element of partisan rancour in this description is no mystery; to be so outshone in popular esteem by Lula has gone hard with his predecessor. But more moderately expressed, the basic analogy is not uncommon, and can be heard among those who respect the memory of Vargas, as well as those who detest it.

Viewed historically, however, comparisons with Vargas, let alone Perón, miss the mark. The differences between their forms of rule and Lula's are fundamental. Not that the great practitioners of populism in Brazil and Argentina much resembled each other. Vargas's rhetoric was paternalist and sentimental, Perón's rousing and aggressive, and their relationship to the masses was quite distinct. Vargas built his power on an incorporation of newly urbanized workers into the political system, as passive beneficiaries of his care, with a protective labour law and a gelded unionization from above. Perón galvanized them as active combatants against oligarchic power, mobilizing proletarian energies in a trade-union militancy that outlived him. The one appealed to lachrymose images of 'the people', while the other called up the anger of *los descamisados*—the local *sansculottes*, lacking shirts rather than breeches.

---

17 'Para onde vamos?', *Estado de S. Paulo*, 1 November 2009.

Lula's exercise of power has involved none of this. His rise was based on a trade-union movement and political party far more modern and democratic than anything Vargas or Perón ever envisaged. But by the time he won the presidency at his fourth attempt, the PT had been largely reduced to an electoral machine. In power, Lula neither mobilized nor even incorporated the electorate that acclaimed him. No new structural forms gave shape to popular life. The signature of his rule was, if anything, demobilization. The trade-unions organized over 30 per cent of the formal labour-force in the eighties, when he made his name as their most gifted leader. Today they number 17 per cent. The decline preceded his period in office, but was not altered by it. Even the *imposto sindical* dating back to the fascist-inspired legislation of the Estado Novo, whose deduction and distribution of dues by the state was long and rightly viewed by the PT as a mechanism for sapping union activism, and whose abolition was a key demand of the early eighties, has been left untouched. Nor, on the other side of the ledger, have the forms of clientelism characteristic of classic populism been reproduced. The Bolsa Família is administered impersonally, clean of capillary systems of patronage. The pattern of rule is quite distinct.

A second interpretation looks to a different parallel. The political scientist André Singer, press secretary to Lula in his first mandate but an independent and original mind, has pivoted a striking analysis of Lulismo on the psychology of the Brazilian poor.[18] This he argues, is a sub-proletariat, comprising nearly half—48 per cent—of the population, that is moved by two principal emotions: hope that the state might moderate inequality, and fear that social movements might create disorder. On

---

18 André Singer, 'Raízes Sociais e Ideológicas do Lulismo', *Novos Estudos* 85, November 2009, pp. 83–102.

Singer's reading, *instability* is a menacing spectre for the poor, whatever form it takes—armed struggle, price inflation or industrial action. So long as the Left failed to understand this, the Right captured their votes for conservatism. In 1989, Lula won every other segment of the electorate, but Collor, brandishing the danger of anarchy, swept the poor to gain a comfortable victory. In 1994 and 1998, Cardoso's throttling of inflation ensured him a still larger margin of the popular vote. In 2002, Lula finally grasped that it was not just contractors and bankers who needed reassurance that he would not do anything unduly radical in power, but—even more crucially—street vendors and slum-dwellers too. It was only in 2006, however, that a complete reversal of allegiances was sealed, as the middle class abandoned him, while the sub-proletariat voted *en masse* for him as never before. When he first ran for office in 1989, Lula took 51.7 per cent of the electorate in the prosperous South of the country, and 29.5 per cent in the famished North-East; in 2006, he lost the South at 46.5 per cent, and swept the North-East with 77.1 per cent.[19]

The economic orthodoxy of Lula's first term, and lesser but continuing caution of his second, were thus more than simple concessions to capital. They answered to the needs of the poor, who unlike workers in formal employment, have no defence against inflation, and dislike strikes even more than the rich, as a threat to daily life. So, coming after Cardoso, Lula cut inflation still further, while also promoting popular consumption,

---

19 For regional breakdowns of the vote, see Wendy Hunter, *The Transformation of the Workers' Party In Brazil, 1989–2009*, Cambridge 2010, p. 170. Historically, as Victor Nunes Leal pointed out already in 1949 in his famous study, *Coronelismo, enxada e voto*, once in power all governments have tended to increase their votes in the North-East. But the scale of Lula's triumph in the region, repeated by Dilma in 2010, far exceeds this traditional effect.

pioneering a 'new ideological road' with a project combining price stability and expansion of the internal market. In this, Singer suggests, he displayed his sensitivity both to the temperament of the masses and to the political culture of the country at large, each in their own way marked by a long Brazilian tradition of conflict-avoidance. Vargas too, until he was under siege at the end, had generally embodied that trait. In certain respects, then—his ability to square the concerns of capital and labour; to exploit favourable external circumstances for internal development; to assert national interests; and above all, to make a connexion with previously inarticulate masses—Lula can indeed thus be regarded as Vargas's heir, offering a potent blend of authority and protection as the 'father of the poor' had once done. But in other ways, his popular roots as a penniless immigrant from the North-East, and unimpeachably democratic commitments, gave him far greater legitimacy and credibility as a defender of the people than a wealthy rancher from the South, who did nothing to alleviate rural misery, could ever possess. Lula did not see himself as a descendant of Vargas. The president with whom he identified was Kubitschek, the builder of Brasília, another optimist who had never willingly made an enemy.

For Singer, however, comparison with a much more famous ruler is in order. Might not Lula have become the Brazilian Roosevelt? The genius of FDR—so his argument goes—was to transform the political landscape with a package of reforms that would eventually lift millions of hard-pressed workers and pinched employees, not to speak of those made jobless by the slump, into the ranks of the post-war American middle class. Any party that sets in motion upward social mobility on such a scale will dominate the scene for a long time to come, as the Democrats did once the New Deal was under way, though eventually the opposition will adjust to the change and compete on the same terrain, as Eisenhower would do in 1952. Presiding over comparable changes, Lula's victories in 2002 and 2006 can be mapped with uncanny closeness onto Roosevelt's of 1932 and 1936: first a large majority, then an avalanche, the popular classes pouring out for the president as the respectable classes turned against him. In prospect could be a Brazilian political cycle equally long, driven by the same dynamics of social ascent.[20]

Glances in the mirror at resemblances with FDR are not new in Brazil. Cardoso also liked to compare his project with that of the Democratic coalition mustered to the North. Lula may come closer, but the contrasts between the New Deal and his intendancy are still plain. Roosevelt's social reforms were introduced under pressure from below, in a wave of explosive strikes and rolling unionization. Organized labour became a formidable force from 1934 onwards, which he had to court as well as control. No such industrial militancy either sustained or challenged Lula—the rural landless attempting the second were much too weak, the MST easily marginalized by him. Vice versa, where Roosevelt confronted a deep slump which the New Deal never really overcame, and was rescued from its failure only by the onset of the Second World War, Lula rode the crest of a commodities boom, in a time of increasing prosperity. Differing in their luck, they differed completely in style too: the patrician who rejoiced in the hatred of his enemies, and the labourer who wanted none, could hardly form a greater contrast. Were the ultimate upshot of their mandates to be the same, there would seem little immediate connexion between causes and effects.

---

20 For this analysis, see 'A História e seus Ardis—O Lulismo posto à prova em 2010', *Folha de S.Paulo*, 19 September 2010, and 'O Lulismo e Seu Futuro', *Piauí* 49, October 2010, pp. 62–6.

Still, in one point there could be thought a certain likeness. The intensity of the animus against Roosevelt in conservative circles, up to the outbreak of the War, was out of all proportion to the actual policies of his administration. Much the same anomaly was to recur in Brazil, where Lula's aversion to conflict was not reciprocated. Anyone whose impressions of his government came from the business press abroad would get a shock from exposure to the local media. Virtually from the start *The Economist* and *Financial Times* purred with admiration for the market-friendly policies and constructive outlook of Lula's presidency, regularly contrasted with the demagogy and irresponsibility of Chavez's regime in Venezuela: no praise was too high for the statesman who put Brazil on a steady path to capitalist stability and prosperity. Readers of the *Folha* or *Estadão*, not to speak of *Veja*, were living in a different world. Typically, in their columns, Brazil was being misgoverned by a crude would-be caudillo without the faintest understanding of economic principles or respect for civil liberties, a standing threat to democracy and property alike.

The degree of venom directed at Lula bore little or no relation to anything he was actually doing. Behind it lay other and deeper grievances. For the media, Lula's popularity meant a loss of power. Traditionally, since the end of military rule, it was in practice the owners of the press and television who selected candidates and determined the outcome of elections. If the most notorious case was the backing of Collor by the *Globo* empire, the coronation of Cardoso by the press, before he had even thrown his hat into the ring, was scarcely less impressive. Lula's direct rapport with the masses broke this circuit, cutting out the media's role in shaping the political scene. For the first time, a ruler did not depend on his proprietors, and they hated him for this. The ferocity of the ensuing campaigns against Lula could not have been sustained, however, without a sympathetic audience. That lay in the traditional middle classes of the country, principally but not exclusively based in the big cities, above all São Paulo. The reason for the hostility to him within this stratum was not loss of power, which it had never really possessed, but of status. Not only was the president now an uneducated ex-worker whose poor grammar was legend, but under his aegis maids and guards and handymen, indeed potentially riff-raff of any kind, were now acquiring consumer goods hitherto the preserve of the educated, and getting above themselves in daily life. To a good many in the middle class, all this grated acutely: the rise of trade-unionists and servants meant they were coming down in the world. The result has been an acute outbreak of 'demophobia', as the columnist Elio Gaspari, a spirited critic of it, has dubbed this reaction.[21] The blending of political chagrin among owners and editors with social resentment among readers made for an often vitriolic brew of anti-Lulismo, bizarrely at odds with any objective sense of class interest.

For, far from doing any harm to the propertied (or credentialed), this was a government that greatly benefited them. Never has capital so prospered as under Lula. It is enough to point to the stock market. Between 2002 and 2010, Bovespa outperformed every other bourse in the world, rocketing by 523 per cent; it now represents the third-largest securities-futures-commodities complex on earth.[22] Such huge speculative gains accrued to a modern bourgeoisie, accustomed to gambling on share prices. For more numerous and risk-averse sectors of the middle class,

---

21 See, *inter alia*, 'A demofobia ajuda Lula, como ajudou Vargas', *O Globo*, 26 September 2006.

22 'Uma era de ouro para a Bolsa', *O Globo*, 4 October 2010; *Financial Times* supplement *The New Brazil*, 29 June 2010, p. 30.

sky-high interest rates yielded more than satisfactory returns on simple bank deposits. If social transfers doubled since the eighties, payments on the public debt trebled. Outlays on the *Bolsa Família* totalled a mere 0.5 per cent of GDP. Rentier incomes from the public debt took a massive 6–7 per cent.[23] Fiscal receipts in Brazil are higher than in most other developing countries, at 34 per cent of GDP, largely because of social commitments inscribed in the Constitution of 1988 at the high point of the country's democratization, when the PT was still a rising radical force. But taxes have remained staggeringly regressive. Those living on less than twice the minimum wage lose half their income to the Treasury, those with thirty times the minimum wage a quarter of theirs.[24] In the countryside, the clearing of vast interior areas of scrub for modern agribusiness, proceeding apace under Lula, has left landownership more concentrated today than it was half a century ago.[25] Urban real estate has moved in the same direction.

Official reports, backed by much statistical analysis, and endorsed by sympathetic agencies and journalists abroad, claim not only a major reduction of poverty in Brazil in these years, of which there is no doubt, but a substantial diminution of inequality, with the Gini index falling from an astronomic 0.58 plus at the start of Lula's term towards a merely towering 0.538 at the

---

23 Marcio Pochmann and Guilherme Dias, 'A sociedade pela qual se luta' in *Brasil entre o Passado e o Futuro*, pp. 116–17.

24 *Economist*, 14 April 2007.

25 Agribusiness currently accounts for over 34 per cent of GDP. Some 1.6 million large landowners, in possession of vast tracts of soil, produce 76 per cent of output, 2.5 million small farmers a mere 7 per cent. Even the most upbeat reports confess that 'the occupation of the so-called *cerrado* (savannas) was not a peaceful process: it was violent and unfair, with heavy costs for native populations and migrants from the Northeast': Geraldo Barros, 'The Challenges in Becoming an Agricultural Superpower', in *Brazil as an Economic Superpower*, p. 85.

end of it.[26] In such estimates, from the turning-point of 2005 onwards, the incomes of the poorest decile of the population are purported to have grown at nearly double the rate of those in the top decile. Best of all, some 25 million people have moved into the ranks of the Brazilian middle class, henceforward a majority of the nation.[27] For many commentators, domestic and foreign, this is the most hopeful single development of Lula's presidency. It forms the ideological *pièce de résistance* of glowing accounts of it by boosters like the Latin American editor for *The Economist*, Michael Reid, eager to hold up the new middle class in Brazil as the beacon of a stable capitalist democracy, in the 'battle for the soul' of a 'forgotten continent' against dangerous rabble-rousers and extremists.[28] Much of this acclaim rests on an artifice of official categorization, in which anyone with an income even as low as $1,750 to $7,000 a year—pauperism elsewhere—is classified as 'middle-class', while according to the same schema the uppermost class—the super-elite of Brazilian society—starts at less than twice the median household income of the world's population.[29] Marcio Pochmann, the head of the country's leading institute of applied economic research, has trenchantly remarked that a more accurate description of the much-touted new middle strata would be simply 'the working poor'.[30]

More generally, the belief that inequality in Brazil has

---

26 'Primeiras Análises: Distribuição da Renda entre 1995 e 2009', *Comunicados do IPEA* 63, 5 October 2010, p. 4.

27 Neri, 'Income Policies', p. 232; 'Primeiras Análises', p 16.

28 Michael Reid, *Forgotten Continent: The Battle for Latin America's Soul*, London and New Haven 2007, *passim*; for a trenchant critique, see Tony Wood, 'Latin America Tamed?', *New Left Review* 58, July–August 2009, pp. 135–48.

29 My thanks to Leda Paulani for discussion of the Alice-in-Wonderland character of such classifications.

30 'A Desigualdade no Brasil é Coisa da Sociedade Feudal', *Caros Amigos*, August 2010, p. 14.

significantly declined can only be met with scepticism, since not merely is it based on data for nominal income that—according to standard statistical rules—exclude 'outliers' at the top, i.e. the super-rich, but much more fundamentally ignores capital appreciation and concealment of financial gains at the summit of society. As the leading study of *Declining Inequality in Latin America* itself notes of standard household surveys: 'incomes from property are grossly underestimated'—'if the top incomes ignored by surveys experience a large enough relative increase, then the true dynamics of overall inequality may display a rising trend even when survey-based estimates show the opposite result.'[31] So in Brazil it is estimated that some 10,000–15,000 families receive the lion's share of the $120 billion annual payments of the public debt (the cost of the Bolsa Família is $6–9 billion), in São Paulo CEOs earn more than in New York, London or Hong Kong, while in the last decade millionaires have multiplied as never before.[32] The explosion of the stock market alone should be warning enough against any naivete on this score. The rich are well aware on which side their bread has been buttered. Unlike the 'economic royalists' attacked by Roosevelt, who detested the New Deal, most Brazilian financiers and industrialists have been warm supporters of Lula's government. Capital has not only been more lucid about it than the—true—middle class, but more comfortable with it than with any previous regime. Logically enough, since profits have never been higher.

---

31 Luis López-Calva and Nora Lustig (eds), *Declining Inequality in Latin America. A Decade of Progress?*, Washington DC, 2010, pp. 16, 85. Of this rule, Ricardo Barros, Mirelha de Carvalho, Samuel Franco and Rosane Mendonça, remark in 'Markets, the State and the Dynamics of Inequality in Brazil', their contribution to the volume: 'Brazilian surveys are no exception': p. 134.

32 For comparative salaries of senior managers—chief executives and company directors—in these cities, see *Economist*, 29 January 2011.

For a third interpretation of Lulismo, these must lie at the centre of any realistic analysis of its system of rule. In a series of iconoclastic essays, the sociologist Chico de Oliveira has developed a vision of it in nearly every way antithetical to that of André Singer, with whom he remains on good terms, despite their political differences—one of the historic founders of the PT, he left the party in disgust soon after Singer joined its government. Oliveira does not contest his friend's characterization of the psychology of the poor, nor the improvements in their lot wrought by Lula. The sub-proletariat is as Singer describes it: without resentment of the rich, satisfied with modest and gradual alleviations of their conditions of existence. But his account focusses too narrowly on the relationship between Lula and the mass of his electorate. Missing are two fundamental parameters for an understanding of Lulismo. The first of these is the moment in the world history of capital at which it came to power.[33] Globalization has cut off the possibility of an inclusive project of national development of the kind long sought in Brazil, not least by those like himself. The third industrial revolution, based on molecular-digital advances that erase the boundary between science and technology, requires investments in research and imposes patents that permit no ready transfer of their results to the periphery of the system—least of all in a country like Brazil, where even at the height of developmentalism under Kubitschek in the fifties, investment has never exceeded a low 22 per cent of GDP, and outlays on R&D remain beggarly.

Thus, instead of further industrial advance, the consequence for Brazil of the latest wave of technological revolution has been

---

33 See *Crítica à Razão Dualista—O Ornitorrinco*, São Paulo 2003, pp. 121–50; in English, 'The Duck-Billed Platypus', *New Left Review* 24, November–December 2003, pp. 40–57.

to shift accumulation away from manufactures to financial transactions and natural-resource extraction, with a very rapid growth in the banking sector, where profits are highest, and in mining and agribusiness for export. The former is an involution, diverting investment from production; the latter a regression, taking Brazil back to earlier cycles of reliance on primary commodities for growth. But in coming to terms with capital, it was to the dynamic of these sectors that Lulismo had to adjust. Here lay the second parameter. For the result of doing so was to transform the structures out of which it had emerged—the party and the trade-unions that after 2002 became the apparatus of power on which it rested. The leadership of the CUT, the principal confederation of labour, was put in charge of the country's largest pension fund. The cadres of the PT colonized the federal administration, where a Brazilian president has the right of nomination to over 20,000 well-paid jobs, far more than the spoils system has ever allowed the executive in America. Now all but completely detached from the working class, this stratum was inexorably sucked into the vortex of financialization engulfing markets and bureaucracies alike. Trade-unionists became managers of some of the biggest concentrations of capital in the country, the scene of ferocious struggles for control or expansion between competing predators. Militants became functionaries enjoying, or abusing, every perquisite of office.

As a new logic of accumulation interlocked with a new incrustation of power, a hybrid social layer was formed—Oliveira would famously compare it to the duck-billed platypus, as a sport of the animal kingdom—whose natural habitat was corruption. Lula's electoral base had come to rest among the unorganized poor of the informal economy, and he could not be reproached for that, nor the neo-populism of his relationship to them, unavoidable for Chavez or Kirchner too. But between the leader and the masses lay an apparatus that had become deformed. Missing in Singer's account was a sense of this dark side of Lulismo. What it had achieved was a kind of inverted hegemony.[34] Where for Gramsci, hegemony in a capitalist social order had been the moral ascendancy of the possessing over the labouring classes, securing the consent of the dominated to their own domination, in Lulismo the dominated had as it were reversed the formula, achieving the consent of the dominant to their leadership of society, only to ratify the structures of their own exploitation. Not the United States of the New Deal, but the South Africa of Mandela and Mbeki was a more appropriate analogy, where the iniquities of apartheid had been overthrown and the masters of society were black, but the rule of capital and its miseries were as implacable as ever. The fate of the poor in Brazil had been a kind of apartheid, and Lula had ended that. But equitable or inclusive progress remained out of reach.

To many even of those close in political outlook to Oliveira, this picture is overdrawn, as if the dark side of Lulismo, hard to deny in itself, has in his representation of it become a total eclipse. How has it been received in the PT itself? With scarcely a word. In part, it is often said, because he is so personally liked and respected that no-one—save Delúbio and Dirceu, who sued him for libel before they were indicted—wants to quarrel with him. A very Brazilian cordiality. But then what of the far more favourable analysis offered by Singer? There too, virtually no

---

34 For this development of Oliveira's analysis, see 'Hegemonia às Avessas', *Piauí* 4, January 2007 and 'O Avesso do Avesso', *Piauí* 37, October 2009, both texts now in Francisco de Oliveira, Ruy Braga and Cibele Rizek (eds), *Hegemonia Às Avessas*, São Paulo 2010, pp. 21–7, 369–76. In English, see 'Lula in the Labyrinth', *New Left Review* 42, November–December 2006, pp. 5–22.

reaction. Transformed into a vote-getting machine, the PT has kept most of its militants and increased its mass membership—it currently claims 1.2 million members, of whom 300,000 voted in its last internal election. Over time its social composition has changed along with its electorate, which has moved, if not in step (the party got just 17 per cent of the vote, its highest ever, for the lower house of Congress in 2010), in the same direction as Lula's popular following, its support dwindling in the middle class and soaring among the poor.[35] But in the process it has lost its intellectual wing, and is generally empty of ideas. When the party emerged at the turn of the eighties, the Brazilian intelligentsia was a vital ferment in the mass movements against the military regime of the time, and played a major role in the politics that followed its withdrawal from the scene. A decade later, when Cardoso took the presidency, it split into two camps bitterly ranged against each other—those who supported his regime, and those who opposed it. The PT was the party of opponents, enjoying the talents of a wide array of the country's most gifted intellectuals. Another ten years on, with Lula in power

---

35 In 1996, 30 per cent of PT sympathizers had an income more than ten times the minimum wage, as against 40 per cent with an income under twice the minimum wage. By 2010, the first group made up 4 per cent, the second 85 per cent. See André Singer, 'A Segunda Alma do Partido dos Trabalhadores', *Novos Estudos* 88, November 2010, p. 95. Given 'the paradox that in Brazil the proletariat is middle-class, for the simple reason that below it exists a vast layer of the population deprived of the possibility of participating in class struggle', the PT is now the 'party of the poor': p. 100. For the evolution of the PT as a political organization, see David Samuels, 'From Socialism to Social Democracy. Party Organization and the Transformation of the Workers' Party in Brazil', *Comparative Politics*, November 2004, pp. 999–1024, who stresses both the changing nature of its base in the trade-unions, now much less industrial and more public-sector employee than in the eighties, and the continuity of its relatively democratic internal structure.

disillusionment had set in. *Faute de mieux*, most of its former lights still vote for it, to keep out the Right, but engagement has gone. To all appearances the party could not care less. Does this matter? In the 1960s, Brazilian culture was a brilliant affair, not only before but even under the military: football not yet expatriate, *bossa nova*, experimental theatre, Cinema Novo, an indigenous Marxism to rival any in Europe— philosophy, sociology, literature, *Kulturkritik*. By the time the country emerged from the dictatorship, however, the two forces that had transformed the cultural landscape in the North were already reshaping it in Brazil too: on the one hand, the modern academy, with its bureaucratization of careers and specialization of fields; on the other, the modern fashion and entertainments industry, marketing anything it can touch. Professionalization, commercialization: no culture has escaped their yoke. With them, inevitably, comes depoliticization. But the extent of that varies widely from one society to another. Compared with the Brazil of fifty or thirty years ago, the decline of political energy in cultural life is palpable. Compared with Europe, the grammar of the imaginary can remain vividly political.

In part, this is due to simple continuity of persons and ideas from an earlier epoch, even against a university backdrop duller, if more proficient, than in the past. A moral-intellectual touchstone for the Left, the doyen of Brazilian literary history Antônio Cândido is still a presence at the age of ninety-three. In the next generation, Roberto Schwarz is the finest dialectical critic since Adorno anywhere in the world; Chico Buarque, a perhaps uniquely versatile author at once of songs, plays, and novels; Oliveira, the most original sociological mind in Latin America; Emir Sader, its one radical political thinker of continental vision. Younger figures like Singer or Pochmann are still products of the final stages of the struggle against the dictatorship. In the arts, explosive forms continue to be produced, if now far more liable to neutralization or degradation into entertainment—Paulo Lins's novel *Cidade de Deus* reduced to cinematic pulp by an expert in TV ads; José Padilha descending from the bitter documentary truths of *Bus 174* to gaumont-grade action films. But the maw of the market is not irresistible. The latest literary grenade, Reinaldo Moraes's scabrous novel *Pornopopéia*, which takes it directly as a target, could prove more difficult to digest.

The change in period has found its barometer in what is now the country's best periodical. The monthly *Piauí* was launched in the autumn of 2006, as Lula coasted to his second term. Its editor, Mario Sergio Conti, who comes originally from a Trotskyist left, ran the mass-circulation weekly *Veja*—Brazil's equivalent of *L'Express* or *Der Spiegel*—in the nineties. Quitting towards the end of the decade, he used a pre-negotiated sabbatical to write a full inside account of the way in which the Brazilian media first propelled Collor into the presidency in 1989, and then deposed him in 1992—Conti himself publishing in *Veja* the key scoop that brought him down. In its sheer narrative drive, span of characters high and low, density of detail, and not least dramatic dénouement, *Notícias do Planalto* reads like a documentary from Balzac. Sparing neither proprietors nor commentators nor reporters, it broke the most fundamental taboo of the press. Retrospective complaints about owners by journalists, on occasion yes. Galleries of the journalists themselves? Humbert Wolfe's quip remains off-limits.[36] Before *Notícias* came out, the magnate

---

36   You cannot hope   But seeing what
to bribe or twist,   the man will do
thank God! the   unbribed, there's
British journalist.   no occasion to.

Roberto Civita, head of the media empire which owns *Veja*, who wanted Conti back in his stable, agreed somewhat reluctantly to let him try out a periodical of more intellectual ambition for a smaller readership, without believing it would make him any money. Preparations for the project went ahead, but when Civita saw *Notícias*, he cancelled it on the spot.

Five years later Conti, then working as a broadcaster in Paris, met through mutual friends an heir to one of the greatest banking fortunes in Brazil, João Moreira Salles. A film director of more discriminating temperament than his better-known elder brother Walter, author of such middle-market fare as *Central do Brasil* and *The Motorcycle Diaries,* João's portrait of Lula backstage during the campaign of 2002, *Entreatos*, is a masterpiece of ambiguity, readable equally as an admiring tribute to the candidate's vitality and affability, or a disquieting trailer for the corrosions of power to come. Moreira Salles, who was also thinking of launching a magazine, had heard of Conti's idea, and after talking it over not only agreed to finance it, but—an unusual arrangement for the millionaire proprietor of a journal—to work for it under Conti. He insisted only that it be edited in Rio, as a counter-weight to the excessive concentration of intellectual life in São Paulo once the capital had moved inland. The magazine that issued from this arrangement is a stylish affair, sometimes seen as a kind of tropical *New Yorker*. But, though certainly smart enough, it differs not only in design, printed on matt paper in larger format, but in spirit, as its title indicates. Piauí, one of the poorest states of the North-East, is a byword for backward provincialism, picked as ironic antithesis to Manhattan. Living up unawares to its reputation, in due course the governor of the state descended on the magazine with a substantial escort, and in a very Brazilian scene thanked its editors effusively for conferring such well-merited distinction on it.

Beneath the veneer of worldliness it still affects, what the *New Yorker* delivers today is mostly a sententious conformism. *Piauí* is more mordant and unplaceable. It is enough to compare the gushing portrait of America's ruler offered by the editor of the first (*Introit*: 'This is how it began, the telling of a story that changed America ...'; *Exit*: 'Obama, who had bowed his head in prayer, broke into a broad smile ... Three times we all said amen')[37] with the lethal coverage of Brazil's elite by the second. *Piauí* has developed the matter-of-fact, deadpan profile into an art more ruinous of its subjects than detraction could ever be. Cardoso, Dirceu, Serra have been among the victims, along with Lula's minister of justice, Márcio Thomaz Bastos and Dilma's vice-president, Michel Temer.[38] In the same impassive tone, the magazine has excavated some of the ugliest episodes and niches of public life: financial brawls, congressional shenanigans, legal enormities.

Two exposés stand out as calm engravings of Brazilian equity and justice. In a miniature masterpiece, Moreira Salles detailed the fate of the young caretaker who saw Palocci entering his lacustrine brothel in Brasilia.[39] A twenty-four-year-old from

---

37 David Remnick, *The Bridge: The Life and Rise of Barack Obama*, New York 2010, pp. 3, 578.

38 For portraits of Cardoso, Dirceu, Thomaz Bastos and Serra, see now the collection *Vultos da República. Os melhores perfis políticos da revista* Piauí, São Paulo, 2010. Cardoso says guilelessly of his time in office: 'Neo-liberalism won. But contrary to what people think, against my will', p. 13. For Temer, see Consuelo Dieguez 'A Cara do PMDB', *Piauí 45*, June 2010.

39 'O caseiro: Francenildo dos Santos Costa', *Piauí 25*, October 2008, now in *Vultos da República*, pp. 69–118. There is a striking parallel with the story of the driver whose testimony sealed the fate of Collor, another hapless victim of the *omertà* of the political class: *Notícias do Planalto*, São Paulo 1999, pp. 592–602, 618–20, 681–2.

Piauí, earning $50 a week, his bank account was broken into by
the president of the Federal Savings Bank, one Jorge Mattoso,
fresh from a meeting in the Presidential Palace, in search of
evidence that the boy had been paid for his testimony by the
opposition. Violation of banking secrecy is a crime in Brazil. An
hour later, Mattoso delivered print-outs to Palocci in person at
his residence, showing that $10,000 had been deposited to the
caretaker's account. Palocci ordered the Federal Police, currently holding him under lock and key, to investigate the boy
on suspicion of bribery and false witness. When it emerged
that the money had been paid by his father, the owner of a bus
company who had hitherto refused to acknowledge him, to fend
off any chance of a paternity suit, he had to be released, and the
police brought criminal charges against Palocci and Mattoso
instead. Palocci had to step down as minister, but the attorney-
general reduced the charges against him and four years later the
Supreme Court acquitted him by five votes to four. Today, this
toad squats in power once more, now chief of staff to the new
president. The boy he sought to frame never found work in the
city again.

What of the Supreme Federal Tribunal that absolved Palocci?
Daumier would have been hard pressed to depict it. Supposedly
concerned with constitutional issues alone, it handles—if that
is the right word—some 120,000 cases a year, or 30 a day per
member of the court. Lawyers transact with judges in private,
and on receiving favourable verdicts, have been known—in full
view—to hug, indeed wine and dine, the justices responsible for
them. Of the eleven current members of the Tribunal, eight of
them appointed by Lula, two have been convicted of crimes in
lower courts. One, appointed by Collor (his cousin), made legal
history by guaranteeing immunity to a defendant in advance of

his trial, but was saved from removal by his peers to 'preserve the honour of the court'. Another, a friend of Cardoso, supported the military coup of 1964, and could not even boast a law degree. A third, on casting a crucial vote to acquit Palocci, was thanked by the president in person for assuring 'governability'. Just retired is Eros Grau, once convicted of trafficking in influence, a particular favourite of Lula; dubbed 'Cupid' by colleagues, and author of a fifth-rate pornographic novel, he sought to get an associate onto the court in exchange for a vote to bury the *mensalão*.[40]

Scenes like these, not vestiges of an older oligarchic regime, but part and parcel of the new popular-democratic order, preclude any complacency about the prospects ahead, without abrogating them. Political and judicial criminality in Brazil, however repellent, is still—its apologists can point out—considerably less than in India, China or Russia, the other BRIC powers with which it is now conventional to compare it. Nor, as last year's presidential election showed again, is corruption, although not unnoticed at the polls—it was partly responsible for the contest going to a second round—a major concern of the masses. The victory of Dilma Rousseff was certainly, by proxy, Lula's greatest electoral triumph. A figure scarcely known to the population a few months earlier, who had never before confronted a voter, or possessed a trace of charisma, polled—once anointed by him—close to Lula's own scores, with a thumping second round majority of 56 per cent: three million less votes than he won in 2006, three million more than in 2002. In Congress, where the PT for the first time became the largest party, and in the Senate, where it also made big gains, she commands majorities

---

40 For all of this, see the devastating two-part exposé by Luiz Maklouf Carvalho, '*Data Venia*, O Supremo' and 'O Supremo, *Quosque Tandem*?', in *Piauí* 47 and 48, August and September 2010, pp. 36–46 and 34–41.

Lula himself never enjoyed—support of over two-thirds of the legislature in each house.

Dilma owes her ascent to the vacuum around the presidency left by the scandals that eliminated Palocci and Dirceu as successors. After their fall, she had three advantages over any other possible contender. She was not a product of the PT, which she only joined in 2000, so lacked any base in the party, from which Lula—publicly at least—had kept his distance once in the Planalto, and therefore posed no threat to him. She was good at something he was not—administration: as minister of energy she had ensured the country did not suffer the blackouts that had so damaged Cardoso's standing in his second term. Finally, she was a woman, around whom it was much easier to wrap the warmth of his own charisma than it would have been a man. A colleague had described the relationship between them, when she became his chief of staff, as not unlike that of father to daughter.[41] In fact they are contemporaries—she is only two years younger than Lula—but the joint campaign they ran in 2010 would have been much more awkward with a male candidate.

In trajectory, not to speak of temperament, the contrasts between them are marked. Dilma comes from an upper-middle-class family. Her father was a Bulgarian Communist who emigrated to Latin America in the thirties and did well in real estate in Belo Horizonte. Sent to good local schools, with private French and piano lessons at home, she was seventeen when the military seized power in Brazil. At nineteen she was in a revolutionary underground carrying out armed actions in and around the city. Moving to Rio in 1968, she was involved in

---

41 See Luiz Maklouf Carvalho, 'As armas e os barões' and 'Dilma Rousseff da prisão ao poder', the best accounts of her career so far, in *Vultos da República*, pp. 161–2.

one of the most famous raids of the time—the expropriation of a chest containing two and a half million dollars from the mistress of the most corrupt of all governors of São Paulo, Adhemar de Barros. In 1970 she was caught in São Paulo, tortured, and jailed for three years. On her release she moved south to Porto Alegre, where her companion in the underground, now her husband, was imprisoned. When the dictatorship loosened in the late seventies, she got a job in the statistical bureau of Rio Grande do Sul, re-entering political life affiliated to the party led by Lula's chief rival on the left in the eighties, Lionel Brizola, and gradually moving up to become Secretary for Energy under a PT Governor. There Lula noticed her technical capabilities in 2002, and brought her to Brasília as minister of mines and energy. In political background a guerrilla rather than a trade-union leader, Dilma, though highly controlled, is more explosive in character than Lula. Observing the way each handled disputes in the energy sector, a leading participant has commented: 'He enjoys them like a spectator of a ping-pong game; her style is to hurl the racket.' No one doubts her toughness.

Of her convictions today, there can be less certainty. Dilma came to prominence under Lula during the more radical phase of his government, so in neo-liberal perception is associated with dangers of an insidious statism and nationalism. There is no question that she has robustly defended the regalian rights of the Brazilian state to the reportedly huge deep-sea oil deposits off the country's coast, which multinational companies and domestic capital have been eying hungrily. She has promised not only an expansion of the housing and infrastructural programmes begun under Lula, but—a major new commitment—universal health coverage for the population. At her inauguration, she went out of her way to pay tribute to the comrades who had fought the dictatorship as she had done, and fallen in the battle against it. But in restoring Palocci to power as chief of staff, and replacing Amorim as foreign minister with a complaisant envoy to Washington, her cabinet is designed to reassure business and the United States that they have little to fear from the new administration.[42] Holding down the minimum wage, hiking interest rates, and promising tighter controls on public spending, her first measures look not unlike the orthodox policies of Lula's first years in power.

Might the same trajectory, curving towards radicalization in a subsequent phase, be repeated? Or is the stock of readily available reforms exhausted? By common consent, steady GDP growth of at least 4.5 per cent a year is required to extend the social achievements of Lula's presidency. Though by Chinese or Indian standards this is a modest target, it exceeds the average Brazilian performance so far this century. Buoyant as it is at the moment, the economy is dogged by three underlying problems. Its savings rate remains extremely low at a mere 17 per cent of national income, less than half that of India, and a third that of China; so investment has stagnated at under 20 per cent, spending on R&D at 1 per cent, of GDP.[43] Brazilian interest rates, on the other hand—currently over 11 per cent—have long been the highest of any major economy. Designed to curb inflation and attract the foreign capital needed to eke out domestic savings,

---

42 'Investors', the *Economist* explained, 'will pay close attention to Antonio Palocci, who oversaw Lula's embrace of market-friendly policies as his first finance minister': 6 November 2010. 'If Ms Rousseff chooses him to be her chief of staff, or best of all, returns him to the finance ministry, her standing with businessfolk will soar'. Naturally, in their coverage of Brazil, its correspondents breathed not a word of Palocci's *déboires* by the Lago Sul.

43 For comparative data, see Martin Wolf, 'Must Try Harder', *Financial Times* supplement *The New Brazil*, 29 June 2010, p.11.

these rates, once combined with export gains and quantitative easing in the US, have driven up the *real* to perilous heights: doubling in value against the dollar under Lula.

Finally, Brazilian trade has become steadily more dependent on agribusiness and mining, where the largest concentrations of domestic capital are to be found, while industry, where multinationals control the most important (automobile) sector, has receded. Between 2002 and 2009, the share of manufactures in Brazilian exports dropped from 55 to 44 per cent, while that of raw materials soared from 28 to 41 per cent.[44] China, responsible for so much of the prosperity of the Lula years, when it became the country's largest trade partner—by 2009 buying eighteen times the value of the commodities it purchased from Brazil at the start of the century—is now threatening to swamp it with low-cost manufactures, whose import from the PRC rocketed 60 per cent last year. Historically, countries have achieved high living standards without wide-ranging industrialization, but these have been sparsely populated settler or sylvan societies with high educational levels—Australia, New Zealand, Finland—exhibiting nothing like Brazil's measures of poverty or demographic profile. Against these can be set Brazil's vast cornucopia of natural resources—as much spare farmland as the US and Russia put together, as much renewable water as the whole of Asia, oil reserves floating the largest IPO in history—and its impressive record of state-led enterprise, to which the country owes its steel and aircraft industries, its breakthroughs in tropical agriculture, and its petroleum giant. The opportunities for faster growth are certainly no less than the obstacles to it.

---

44 'Brazilian Factories Tested by Chinese Imports', *Financial Times*, 31 January 2011.

What balance sheet of the Brazilian experience set in motion under Lula, and still unfolding, is at this point possible? Viewed as a period in the political economy of Brazil, it can be regarded as contiguous with that of Cardoso, a development within the same matrix.[45] Viewed as a social process, on the other hand, it has marked a distinct break. Among the conditions of that change have been external conditions that were unusually propitious. This was a time in which South America as a whole has been the scene of a shift to the left setting it apart from the rest of the world.[46] Chávez came to power in Venezuela well before, Kirchner in Argentina just after, Lula in Brazil. The following year, Tabaré Vázquez took Uruguay for the Frente Amplio. Thereafter, in succession, Bolivia, Ecuador and Paraguay elected the most radical presidents in their history. What lay behind this global exception were two distinguishing features of the region. Under supervision from Chicago and Harvard, it was here that neo-liberalism was first introduced and shock therapy applied, by Pinochet in Chile and Sanchez de Lozada in Bolivia well before these took off further north, and privatizations by Menem in Argentina outdid those in Russia.

But it was here too that the first popular uprising against a neo-liberal package erupted, in the *Caracazo* that led to the end of the old order in Venezuela. Economically—Venezuela is the exception, since they were never successfully imposed in the

---

45 For a well-documented—and approving—exposition of the continuities of economic model across the Cardoso and Lula administrations, see Peter Kingstone and Aldo Ponce, 'From Cardoso to Lula: the Triumph of Pragmatism in Brazil', in Kurt Weyland, Raúl Madrid and Wendy Hunter (eds), *Leftist Governments in Latin America: Successes and Shortcomings*, Cambridge 2011, pp. 98–123.

46 The commanding analysis is Emir Sader, 'The Weakest Link? Neoliberalism in Latin America', *New Left Review* 52, July–August 2008, pp. 5–31.

first place—the parameters of the neo-liberal period were rarely rolled back. But they were never popular, and their architects fell into a political discredit that their northern counterparts, even today mostly unscathed by 2008, have escaped. Here the other particularity of the region kicked in. Latin America is the only part of the world to have produced a century of radical revolts against the established order, stretching back in more or less unbroken sequence to the Mexican Revolution of 1910. In different periods these have taken different forms, but their underlying impetus has been much the same, and despite every kind of repression or deflection, has yet to be checked: armed insurrections in El Salvador and Brazil in the twenties; popular front in Chile, peasant rising in Peru in the thirties; military Jacobinism in Argentina in the forties; worker militias in Bolivia, expropriations in Guatemala, revolution in Cuba in the fifties; guerrillas from Colombia to Uruguay in the sixties; victory at the polls in Chile, on the streets in Nicaragua in the seventies; civil wars in Central America in the eighties; overthrow of the oligarchy in Venezuela in the nineties. The electoral harvest of the new century is a mutation out of the same soil.

The generation that came to power in this period had lived through two kinds of defeat: by the military dictatorships that crushed the left in the aftermath of the Cuban Revolution, and by the free market systems that were in part the price, in part the upshot, of democratization. The two formed a single legacy. Earlier forms of radicalism, political or economic, were ruled out of court by their succession. But there was little real social adhesion to the neo-liberal regimes for which the generals had paved the way; and when their time ran out, the leaders who followed them respected, pragmatically, the rules they had imposed, but could not altogether bury memories of a more insurgent past, and the loyalties that went with them, still less forget the constituencies excluded from the new order. Venezuela, which never knew a military dictatorship during the high tide of continental counterrevolution, nor—the two absences were closely connected—a neo-liberal stabilization in its wake, was the exception, Chávez operating in other, more under-determined conditions.

Brazil, on the other hand, can be taken as the epitome of the general pattern. For most of its history, by reason of language, size and geography, the country was rather isolated from the rest of Latin America. As late as the mid sixties, Brazilian intellectuals were more likely to have spent time in France than visited any neighbouring society. The common experiences of underground work, imprisonment or exile—Cuba and Mexico chief refuges— once the military tyrannies took over, changed this. For the first time, politically active Brazilians were connected in a continental network with their opposite numbers in the Spanish-speaking Americas. The solidarities of that period continue to inhabit the political landscape today among governments of the Left, cradling Brazil within a hospitable environment. In a regional dialectic, the differences between them have often worked to mutual advantage, Lula extending a mantle of protective friendship to regimes—Bolivia, Venezuela, Ecuador—more radical than his own, while benefiting in international opinion from favourable comparison of his moderation to their extremism.

In the same period, the international context has been as benign for Brazil as the regional setting. On the one hand, the United States lost concentration as continental overlord once it declared War on Terror in the Middle East and beyond. With Iraq, Afghanistan, Yemen, Pakistan, Egypt as front-lines of American strategy, there was little attention to spare for the hemisphere. Bush paid one distracted visit to Brasília, and Obama is making another in March. There will be effusive greetings for the first mulatto president of the United States, as Brazilians see him, who had their own long ago. But no-one thinks the call will be much more than ceremonial. The traditional mechanisms of supervision, still in working order in Cardoso's time, have rusted. Not just the military expeditions to the Orient of the last decade, but the financial bubble preceding and accompanying them, have tilted the relationship between the two states in Brazil's favour. Once the American economy became dependent on ever greater injections of cheap money—first, under Clinton and Bush very low interest rates, now under Obama quantitative easing—the external capital needed to keep the Brazilian economy growing became more and more available, at less and less cost. If the flow now even risks overwhelming the *real,* that is only another, perverse sign of the alteration in their respective positions. For Brazil, still more decisive has been the ascent of China as a countervailing economic power, the principal market for its two leading exports, soya and iron ore, and the mainstay of its trade balance. The long Chinese boom has affected virtually every part of the world. But Brazil is arguably the country where it has made the greatest difference. As the US dipped and the PRC swelled, the winds allowed passage to a new social direction.

Its upshot remains, for the moment, undecidable. There is no doubt that an emancipation has occurred. But just there, might Brazilian history supply an unsettling analogy? In the late nineteenth century, slavery was abolished in Brazil virtually without bloodshed, in contrast to the slaughter with which its end, not even originally intended, was accompanied in the United States. But it was not only the cost in lives that was low. The cost in property was also low, for emancipation came late, when the slave population was dwindling, and the slave economy in advanced stages of decline. It was not a purely elite affair; popular abolitionism took many an imaginative initiative in its quietus.[47] But when it came, slave-owners were not all ruined, and slaves gained legal freedom alone. Socially, the after-effects were modest: principally, increased white immigration from Europe.

Could there be, *mutatis mutandis*, some resemblance with the Bolsa Família, *crédito consignado*, minimum wage? Lula liked to say—it became a kind of motto—'It's cheap and easy to look after the poor'.[48] Uplifting, or disturbing words? In their moral ambiguity might lie one kind of epitaph on his rule. Compared with his predecessors, he had the imagination, born of social identification, to see that the Brazilian state could afford to be more generous to the least well-off, in ways that have made a substantial difference to their lives. But these concessions have come at no cost to the rich or comfortably off, who in any absolute reckoning have done even better—far better—during these years. Does that really matter, it can be asked—isn't this just the definition of the most desirable of all economic outcomes, a Pareto optimum? Were the pace of growth to falter, however, as the wave of emancipation did a century ago, the descendants of slaves might live out an aftermath not so different. From the time of its adoption, just after slavery was gone, the Comtean motto inscribed on the banner of the nation—*Ordem e Progresso*—has mostly been a tattered hope fluttering in the wind. Progress

---

47 For what is still the best overview, see Seymour Drescher, 'Brazilian Abolition in Comparative Perspective', *Hispanic American Historical Review*, 1988, pp. 429–60.

48 '*A coisa mais fácil para um presidente é cuidar dos pobres. Não tem nada mais barato do que cuidar dos pobres*': speech to departing ministers, 31 March 2010. By then it had become virtually a stock phrase, repeated on many occasions.

without conflict; distribution without redistribution. How common are they, historically?

Yet perhaps this time it will not be the same. The last decade has not seen any mobilization of the popular classes in Brazil. The fear of disorder, and acceptance of hierarchy, which still set them apart within Latin America, are legacies of slavery. But though material betterment is not social empowerment, there are circumstances in which one can lead to the other. The sheer electoral weight of the poor, juxtaposed against the sheer scale of economic inequality, not to speak of political injustice, make of Brazil a democracy unlike any society in the North, even those where class tensions were once highest, or the labour movement strongest. The contradiction between the two magnitudes has only just begun to work itself out. Should passive improvement ever become active intervention, the story would have another ending.

4

DILMA

2016

The BRICs are in trouble. For a season the dynamos of international growth, while the West was mired in the worst financial crisis and recession since the Depression, they are now the leading source of anxiety in the headquarters of the IMF and the World Bank. China, above all, because of its weight in the global economy: slowing output and a Himalaya of debt. Russia: under siege, oil prices falling and sanctions biting. India: holding up best, but unsettling statistical revisions. South Africa: in free fall. Political tensions are rising in each: Xi and Putin battening down unrest with force, Modi thrashed at the polls in Delhi, Zuma disgraced within his own party. Nowhere, however, have economic and political crises fused so explosively as in Brazil, whose streets have in the past year seen more protestors than the rest of the world combined.

Picked by Lula to succeed him, the former guerrilla Dilma Rousseff who had become his chief of staff won the presidency

in 2010 with a majority nearly as sweeping as his own. Four
years later, she was re-elected, this time with a much smaller
margin of victory, a 3 per cent lead over her opponent Aécio
Neves, governor of Minas Gerais, in a result marked by a greater
regional polarization than ever before. The industrialized South
and South-East swung heavily against her, the North-East
delivering an even larger landslide for her—72 per cent—than
in 2010. But overall it was a clear-cut win, comparable in size
to that of Mitterrand over Giscard, and a good deal larger, not
to speak cleaner, than that of Kennedy over Nixon. In January
2015 Dilma began her second presidency.

Within three months, huge demonstrations packed the
streets of the country's major cities, at least two million strong,
demanding her ouster. In Congress, the PSDB and its allies,
emboldened by polls showing her popularity had fallen to single
figures, moved to impeach her. On May Day, she was unable
even to give a traditional televised address to the nation. The
PT, which had long enjoyed far the highest level of approval
in Brazil, became the most unpopular party in the country. In
private, Lula could be heard lamenting: 'We won the election.
The following day we lost it'. Many militants wondered if the
party would survive at all.

How had it come to this? In the last year of Lula's rule, when
the global economy was still gripped by the aftermath of the
financial crash of 2008, the Brazilian economy grew 7.5 per
cent. On taking office as his successor, Dilma tightened policy
against risks of over-heating, to the satisfaction of the financial
press, in what looked like the kind of reinsurance policy Lula had
taken out at the start of his first term. But as growth fell sharply,
and world financial skies darkened once more, the government
changed course, with a package of measures to prime investment

for sustained development. Interest rates were lowered, payroll taxes cut, and electricity costs reduced; state banks increased loans to the private sector, the currency was devalued and limited control of capital movements imposed.[1] On the heels of this stimulus, half-way through her presidency Dilma enjoyed an approval rating of 75 per cent.

But far from picking up, the economy slowed from an already mediocre 2.75 per cent in 2011 to a mere 1 per cent in 2012, and with inflation by then at over 6 per cent, in April 2013 the Central Bank abruptly raised interest rates, undercutting the 'new economic matrix' of Guido Mantega, the finance minister. Two months later the country was swept by a wave of mass protests, triggered by higher bus fares in São Paulo and Rio but quickly escalating into generalized expressions of discontent with the quality of public services and, fanned by the media, hostility to an incompetent state. Overnight, approval of the government fell by half. In response, it beat a retreat, starting cautionary reductions in public spending and allowing interest rates to rise again. Growth fell further—it would be nil in 2014—but employment and wages remained stable. At the end of her first term Dilma waged a defiant campaign for re-election, assuring

---

1   André Singer has written the commanding analysis of this set of measures, and their fate, in 'Cutucando onças com varas curtas', *Novos Estudos* 102, July 2015, pp. 30–67. The essay can be read as an epilogue to his fundamental study of the trajectory of the PT, *Os sentidos do Lulismo. Reforma gradual e pacto conservador*, São Paulo 2012, which traces the change in its electorate after 2005, as it lost its support in the middle class and won the allegiance of the poor, who had once, in fear of disorder, voted against it. Exemplary in his combination of critical sobriety and loyalty to it, Singer is the party's finest intellectual—arguably, indeed, the most impressive social thinker of his generation in Latin America. Press secretary to Lula in his first presidency, since he became a university teacher he has been mentally discarded by the PT, which has shown no interest in his work on it.

voters that as president she would continue to give priority to improvement in the living standards of working people, and attacking her PSDB opponent for planning to reverse the social gains of PT rule by slashing social benefits and hitting the poor. In the face of a continuous ideological barrage against her in the press, it was enough to give her victory.

No sooner re-elected, and before her second term had even formally begun, Dilma reversed course. A spell of austerity, she abruptly explained, was required. The architect of the 'new economic matrix' was dismissed, and the Chicago-trained head of the asset management division of Brazil's second-largest private bank installed at the Finance Ministry, with a mandate to curb inflation and restore confidence. The imperatives now were to cut social spending, curtail credit from public banks, auction state property and raise taxes to bring the budget back into primary surplus. Soon the Central Bank had hiked interest rates to 14.25 per cent. Since the economy had already stalled in 2014, the effect of this pro-cyclical package was to plunge the country into a full-blown recession—investment declining, wages falling and unemployment more than doubling. As GDP contracted, fiscal receipts fell, worsening the deficit and public debt. No government's ratings could have withstood the speed of this deterioration. But the melt-down of Dilma's popularity was not just the predictable result of its impact on ordinary living standards. It was also, more painfully, the price of her abdication from the promises on which she was elected. Overwhelmingly, the reaction among her voters was that her victory was an *estelionato* —an embezzlement: cheating her supporters to steal the clothes of her opponents. Not just disillusion, but anger followed.

The roots of this debacle lay half-hidden in the soil of the PT's model of growth itself. Its success had always relied on two kinds of nitrogen: a super-cycle of commodity prices, and a domestic consumption boom. Between 2005 and 2011, the terms of trade for Brazil improved by a third, as demand for its raw materials from China and elsewhere increased the value of its principal exports and the volume of tax receipts for social expenditures. By the end of Lula's second term, the share of primary commodities in the Brazilian export package had jumped from 28 to 41 per cent, while manufactures had fallen from 55 to 44 per cent; by the end of Dilma's first term, raw materials accounted for over half the value of all exports. But from 2011 onwards the prices of the country's leading tradable goods collapsed—iron ore dropped from $180 to $55 a ton, soya from $18 to $8 a bushel, crude oil from $140 to $50 a barrel. Compounding the end of the overseas bonanza, domestic consumption hit the buffers. Throughout its rule, the PT's core strategy had been to expand home demand by increasing popular purchasing power. That was achieved, not only by raising the minimum wage and making cash transfers to the poor—the Bolsa Família—but with a massive injection of consumer credit. Over the decade from 2005 to 2015, total debt owed by the private sector increased from 43 to 93 per cent of GDP, with consumer loans running at double the level of neighbouring countries. By the time Dilma was re-elected in late 2014, interest payments on household credit were absorbing over a fifth of average disposable income.[2] Along with the exhaustion of the commodity boom, the consumer spree was no longer sustainable. The two engines of growth had sputtered to a halt.

In 2011 the aim of Mantega's 'new economic matrix' was to kick-start the economy back to life by lifting investment. But his means of doing so had narrowed. State banks had been

---

2   *Financial Times*, 31 January 2011.

steadily increasing their share of loan capital, from a third to a half of all credit since he took over in 2006—alone, the portfolio of the government's development bank BNDES rose seven-fold after 2007. Offering preferential rates to leading companies that came to a much larger subsidy than outlays to poor families, the 'Bolsa Empresarial' cost the treasury about double the Bolsa Família.[3] Favourable to large commodity and construction firms, this direct expansion of public banking was anathema to an urban middle class in an increasingly violent anti-PT mood, the local media—amplified by the business press in London and New York—vituperating the dangers of statism. So switching direction, Mantega sought to boost private-sector investment by tax concessions and lower interest rates, at the cost of a reduction in public infrastructural investment, and to help manufacturers with a devaluation of the *real*. But Brazilian industry was wooed in vain. Structurally, finance is a much stronger force in the land. The combined capitalization of its two largest private banks, Itaú and Bradesco, is now twice that of Petrobras and Vale, its two biggest extractive firms, and far sounder. The fortunes of these and other banks have been made from the highest long-term interest regime in the world—crippling for investors, manna for rentiers—and staggering spreads between deposits and loans, borrowers paying anything from five to twenty times the cost of the same money to lenders. Flanking this complex is the sixth-largest bloc of mutual and pension funds in the world, not to speak of the biggest private investment bank in Latin America, and a swarm of private-equity and hedge funds.

In the belief that this would rally manufacturers to its side, the government confronted the banks by forcing interest rates

---

3 *Economist*, 19 October 2013; 18 October 2014.

down to an unprecedented real level of 2 per cent by the end of 2012. In São Paulo the employers federation briefly expressed its appreciation of the change, before hanging out flags in support of the anti-statist marchers on June 2013. Industrialists were happy to reap high profits from the positive-sum period of growth under Lula, in which virtually every social group saw its position improve. But when this ended under Dilma, and strikes flared up, they were unmoved by the favours granted them. Not only were big companies in the real economy, like their counterparts in the North, themselves often long on financial holdings negatively affected by any sharp pressure on rentier revenues, and for that reason not readily detachable from banks or funds. But as a social group most manufacturers formed part of an upper middle class much more numerous, vocal and politicized than the ranks of businessmen proper, with greater ideological and communication capacity in society at large. The rabid hostility of this stratum to the PT inevitably lapped over them. Between bankers above and professionals below, each committed to bringing down a regime now threatening their common interests, producers lacked significant autonomy.

Against this front, on what support could the PT count? The trade-unions, if somewhat more active under Dilma, were a shadow of their combative past. The poor remained passive beneficiaries of PT rule, which had never educated or organized, let alone mobilized, them as a collective force. Social movements—of the landless, or the homeless—had been kept at a distance. Intellectuals were marginalized. But not only had there been no political potentiation of energies from below. The style of the material benefactions of the regime created little solidarity. There was no redistribution of wealth or income: the infamously regressive tax structure bequeathed by Cardoso to

Lula, penalizing the poor to pamper the rich, was left untouched. Distribution there was, appreciably raising the living standards of the least well-off, but it was individualized in form. With the Bolsa Família, disbursements to mothers of school-age children, this could not have been otherwise. With increases in the minimum wage, there was an expansion of the number of workers with the *carteira assinada*, entitling them to the rights of formal employment but no increase, if anything a decline, in unionization. Above all, with the arrival of *crédito consignado*— bank loans at high interest rates deducted in advance from wages—private consumption was unleashed without restraint at the expense of public services, which would have cost more. Purchase of electronics, white goods and vehicles was fanned (cars with tax incitements), while clean water, paved roads, efficient buses, acceptable sewers, decent schools and hospitals were neglected. Collective goods had neither ideological nor practical priority. So along with much-needed, genuine improvements in domestic living, consumerism in its deteriorated sense spread downwards through the social hierarchy from a middle class besotted, even by international standards, with its magazines and malls.

How damaging this has been for the PT can be seen in the fate of housing, where collective and individual needs most visibly intersect. For with the consumer bubble came a much more dramatic real estate bubble, in which vast fortunes were made by developers and construction firms, while the price of housing for the majority of those living in big cities soared, and about a tenth of the population lacked any adequate dwellings at all. From 2005 to 2014, credit for real estate speculation and construction increased twenty times over; in São Paulo and Rio prices per square metre quadrupled. In São Paulo, average rents increased 146 per cent in 2010 alone. In the same years six million apartments stood vacant, while seven million families were in need of decent housing.[4] Rather than itself increasing the supply of popular housing, the government funded private contractors to build settlements at a handsome profit in exurban areas, charging rents typically beyond the reach of the poorest layer of the population, and stood by as local authorities launched evictions of those who occupied vacant terrain. In the face of all this, social movements of active solidarity among the homeless have sprung up, now the most important in Brazil: not around, but against the PT.

Lacking any popular counter-force to withstand concerted pressure from the country's elites, Dilma no doubt hoped, after her narrow re-election, that by beating an economic retreat, with an initial belt-tightening like that of Lula's first years in power, she could reproduce the same kind of upturn. But external conditions precluded any comparable outcome. The dance of the commodities has gone, and recovery, whenever it comes, is likely to be subdued. It can be argued that, viewed in context, the extent of current difficulties should not be exaggerated. The country is in a severe recession, GDP falling 3.7 per cent last year, and probably much the same this year. On the other hand, unemployment has yet to reach the levels of France, let alone Spain. Inflation is lower than in Cardoso's last years, and reserves higher. Public debt is half that of Italy, though Brazilian interest rates make the cost of servicing it far greater. The fiscal deficit is below the EU average. All these figures are likely to worsen. Still, the depth of the economic hole does not so far match the

---

4 Guilherme Boulos, *Por que ocupamos? Uma introdução à luta dos sem-teto*, São Paulo 2014, pp. 13–16; *De que lado você está? Reflexões sobre a conjuntura política e urbana no Brazil*, São Paulo 2015, pp. 11–12.

volume of ideological clamour about it: partisan opposition and
neo-liberal fixation have every interest in overstating the plight
of the nation. But that scarcely reduces the scale of the crisis in
which the PT is now floundering, which is not just economic,
but political.

There, the origins of its predicament lie in the structure of the
Brazilian Constitution. Virtually everywhere in Latin America,
presidencies inspired by the US coexist with parliaments modelled on Europe—that is, over-mighty executives on the one
hand, and legislatures elected by proportional representation
of votes, not Anglo-Saxon first-past-the-post distortion of them,
on the other. The typical, if not invariable, result is a presidency
with sweeping administrative powers, whose weak undercarriage
is a party lacking any majority in a parliament with significant
legislative powers. Nowhere else, however, is the divarication
between executive and legislative anything like as pronounced
as in Brazil. This is, above all, because the country has far the
weakest party system in the continent.[5] There, proportional
representation operates with an open list system, in which elec-
tors can choose any candidate from among a host of individuals
nominally standing on the same ticket, in constituencies whose
size can be a million or more. The consequences of this configuration are two-fold. Overwhelmingly, voters pick a politician of
whom they know—or think they know—something, rather than
a party of which they know little or nothing, while politicians,
for their part, need to raise huge sums of money for campaigns

---

5   For lucid early reflections on this, see Scott Mainwaring, 'Brazilian Party
    Underdevelopment in Comparative Perspective', *Political Science Quarterly*,
    Winter 1992–93, pp. 677–707. On the exceptional width of the gap between
    presidential and parliamentary votes, see the table in his *Rethinking Party
    Systems in the Third Wave of Democratization: The Case of Brazil*, Stanford
    1999, p. 30.

to secure voter identification with them.[6] The great majority of parties, whose number has increased with every election—there are twenty-eight in the current Congress—lack any political coherence, let alone discipline. Their purpose is simply to wrest favours from the executive to line their own pockets, passing down a residuum to their constituents to secure re-election, in exchange for supplying their votes to the government in the chamber.

When Brazil emerged from two decades of military dictatorship in the mid eighties, this was a system preserved by a political class shaped under it. Objectively, its function was and is to neutralize the possibility that democracy might lead to the formation of any popular will that could threaten the enormities of Brazilian inequality, by chloroforming voter preferences in a miasma of sub-political contests for venal advantage.[7] Further

---

6 In 1986, the average successful candidate for federal deputy in the state of São Paulo spent $600,000. 'Even allowing for the fact that São Paulo is Brazil's wealthiest state and probably has the most expensive campaigns, these figures are staggering. Consider, for example, that in 1988 the winning candidates for the US House of Representatives spent an average of $393,000': Scott Mainwaring, 'Brazil. Weak Parties, Feckless Democracy', in Scott Mainwaring and Timothy Scully (eds), *Building Democratic Institutions: Party Systems in Latin America*, Stanford 1995, p. 381.

7 This is a leading theme of Kurt Weyland's study, *Democracy without Equity: Failures of Reform in Brazil*, Pittburgh 1996, which showed that military rule was in some respects socially more progressive than the democracy which followed it, up to Collor. Subsequently, Weyland decided that there was something to be said for the arrangements he had once criticized, since 'deficiencies in the quality of Brazilian democracy—especially weak representation and low accountability—help prevent the translation of socioeconomic problems into open political conflict, which could endanger democratic sustainability': a prospect that victory in the Cold War, by eliminating any prospect of socialism, had thankfully reduced, but not altogether banished. See Weyland, 'The Growing Sustainability of Brazil's Low-Quality Democracy', in Frances Hagopian and Scott Mainwaring (eds), *The Third Wave of Democratization in Latin America: Advances and Setbacks*, New York 2005, p. 104.

accentuating the bias of the system is massive geographical malapportionment. All federal systems require some equalization of regional weighting within them, typically involving over-representation in an upper chamber of areas that are smaller and more rural, at the expense of those that are larger and more urbanized, as in the US Senate. Few, however, approach the degree of distortion that its engineers built into the Brazilian system, where the ratio of over-representation between the smallest and largest state in the Senate is 88:1 (in the US it is around 65:1). Not only do the three poorest and most backward macro-regions, which account for two-fifths of the population— haunts of the most traditional caciques dominating the most submissive clienteles—control three quarters of the seats in the upper house of Congress. Uniquely, they command a majority in the lower house, too.[8] Far from correcting the conservative tilt of this system, democratization has increased it, adding new under-populated states that aggravate the imbalance.

In this landscape, unlike any other country in Latin America to emerge from military rule in the eighties, no political parties of significance survived from the period before the dictatorship. Rather, the stage was initially occupied by two forces derived from constructs of the generals: their party of nominal opposition, the MDB, and their party of government, ARENA—mocked at the time as the difference between muttering *sim* and *sim, senhor*. The former eventually renamed itself the PMDB, and most of the latter morphed into a 'Liberal Front', the PFL. After the generals had withdrawn, the first stable government came with Cardoso's presidency in 1994, born of a pact between a spin-off from the PMDB he had helped create, the—nominally

---

8   For state-by-state tabulation of the distortions in the Chamber of Deputies, see Barry Ames, *The Deadlock of Democracy in Brazil*, Ann Arbor 2001, p. 53.

social-democratic, in fact social-liberal—PSDB, whose electorate was in the industrialized South and South-East of the country, and the—nominally liberal, in fact conservative—PFL, whose base lay in the retrograde North-East and North. This was a deal between moderate opponents and traditional ornaments of the dictatorship that assured the executive a consistently large majority in the legislature, in the service of what would become a neo-liberal programme in line with the Washington Consensus of the period. As a presidential candidate, Cardoso—regarded by capital as a guarantee against radicalization—was drenched with money. The well-off knew their friend. The relative cost of his campaigns, in a much poorer country, exceeded Clinton's in the United States. Running against him, Lula was drowned in a torrent of cash. But once in office Cardoso did not in general— though there would be a crucial exception—need money to buy support in Congress, where his coalition with the oligarchic clans of the North-East, while subject to standard jostling over prebends, was not simply one of convenience, but the coming together of natural partners around common objectives. The arrangement was stable, and has in recent years been much praised by Brazilian and Anglophone admirers of Cardoso as a model of 'coalitional presidentialism', touted as a hopeful example to much of the rest of the world, where European or American forms of government are unlikely to take root.[9]

---

9   For perhaps the most egregious version of this literature, see Marcus André Melo and Carlos Pereira, *Making Brazil Work: Checking the President in a Multiparty System*, New York 2013, pp. 4, 13, 158–61. See also Timothy Power, 'Optimism, Pessimism, and Coalitional Presidentialism: Debating the Institutional Design of Brazilian Democracy', *Bulletin of Latin American Research*, No. 1, 2010, pp. 18–33, where coalitional presidentialism is hailed as 'a self-regulating system capable of generating corrective and pre-emptive measures aimed at ensuring governability'.

Still, although the coffers of Cardoso's campaigns were 'clean' in the sense of American money politics, where PACs—now Super-PACs—buy votes, and his coalition was ideologically unforced, once he was elected neither his objectives nor those of his allies could be achieved without reliance on other methods. Both his vice-president, Marco Maciel, and his most powerful ally in Congress, Antônio Carlos Magalhães, were linchpins of the repressive political order in the North-East—one installed as governor by the dictatorship in Pernambuco, the other in Bahía, after both had supported the destruction of democracy in 1964— with no intention of altering traditional ways of running it. ACM, as he liked to be known, famously boasted: 'I win elections with a bag of money in one hand and a whip in the other'.[10] His son Luis Eduardo was Cardoso's favourite politician in Congress, the dauphin scheduled to succeed him, had he not unexpectedly died young. Cardoso himself, who had long maintained that reform of the party system was a priority for Brazil and promised to deliver it, decided as soon as he was in the Planalto that the real priority was to change the constitution so he himself could be elected for a second term. Abandoning any attempt to rationalize or democratize the political order, he presided—here, where it did prove necessary—over straightforward bribing of deputies to purchase the super-majority in Congress required to ram the amendment through.

When Lula was finally elected in 2002, the PT was in a different position. Once he had given reassurances that he would not attack them, and looked as if he would probably win, Lula's

---

10 See Celina Souza, *Constitutional Engineering in Brazil: The Politics of Federalism and Decentralization*, Basingstoke 1997, p. 127, which traces ACM's career and modus operandi in Bahía prior to subsequent mishaps in the Senate: pp. 124–38.

campaign too had been funded by banks and companies, if on nothing like the scale of his predecessor. But in Congress, he had no natural allies of any significance. The PT, for all the moderation of Lula's pitch for the presidency, was regarded by others—and still regarded itself—as a radical party, well to the left of the marshlands composing the overwhelming mass of the legislature. There the PT had no more than a fifth of the deputies, on a vote less than a third of Lula's own. How was it to secure any kind of supportive working majority from this *marais*? The traditional way, practiced on a heroic scale by the first president after the dictatorship, José Sarney, another former servitor of the generals, was to buy support by handing out ministries and sinecures to whoever was most avid and could deliver the largest number of votes in exchange for them—in the first instance, competing factions in what was formally his own party, the catchall PMDB, the largest and most characterless political entity in the country, which a decade later had become the perennial sump into which every rivulet of Brazilian political corruption drained.[11] The classic course for the PT would have been to cut a deal with this creature, by allocating it a major share of cabinet posts and state agencies.

That solution the party—there is dispute as to who in its high command was for and who against it—rejected, fearing that it would install such an ideological dead-weight within the government that a progressive momentum of any kind would be neutered.[12] Instead, the decision was made to stitch together

11 For the critical position occupied by the PMDB in the post-military institutional system, and its influence in shaping the political culture of the country at large, see the penetrating analysis of Marcos Nobre, *Imobilismo em movimento: da abertura democrática ao governo Dilma*, São Paulo 2013, passim.

12 For writers in the *mouvance* of the PSDB today, this was an unpardonable

a patchwork out of the dense array of smaller parties, without conceding them much foothold in the government, but paying them cash for their support in the chamber by way of a solatium. In effect, the PT attempted to compensate for its lack of the kind of partners with whom Cardoso had enjoyed a natural intercourse, and its refusal of the kind of spoils system Sarney had operated, by dispensing a set of material inducements to cooperate at a lower level, and in lesser coinage: monthly wads of money in lieu of major offices of state.

When it broke in 2005, the scandal of the *mensalão* lost Lula the support of his middle-class electorate, and nearly finished his first presidency. Once he survived it to be triumphantly re-elected the following year, the PT had little choice but to fall back on the solution it had sought to avoid. The PMDB entered *en bloc* into the government, with a roster of ministries and key posts in Congress. Far from declining, systemic corruption began to escalate. Not only was the PMDB a byword for plunder of public resources in its strongholds at municipal and state level (for decades it had ceased even to put up a presidential candidate). But by now another honey-pot, beyond any previous imagining, was taking shape with the expansion of Petrobras, the state oil firm, whose activities would at its height amount to 10 per cent of GDP, and market capitalization make it the fourth-largest company in the world. The construction of new refineries, tankers, rigs, offshore platforms, petrochemical

---

break with the best practice of coalitional presidentialism, explicable only by PT pretensions to an improper hegemony in the political system: see Carlos Pereira and Samuel Pessoa, 'PSDB e PT discordam mais sobre alianças do que sobre inclusão', *Folha de S. Paulo*, 11 October 2015. Pessoa was an adviser to Aécio Neves in his Presidential campaign. For a temperate but telling reply, see Carlos Rocha de Barros: 'Atalhos e pedágios', *Folha*, 26 October 2015.

complexes offered vast opportunities for kick-backs, and soon an established scheme was in place. Tenders would be held down by a cartel of the country's leading construction firms, but contracts over-invoiced to put vast sums of money into the pockets of Petrobras directors and the political parties to whom they owed their appointments—bribes in the region of perhaps $3 billion.

Malversation was certainly no novelty in the history of Petrobras, Cardoso preferring to look the other way, and until the spring of 2013 it had enjoyed the customary impunity of wealth and power in Brazil. What changed this were three after-effects of the *mensalão*.

Plea bargaining—the Portuguese term *delação premiada* is less euphemistic: 'reward for delation'—was introduced in Brazil; indefinite preventive imprisonment, or *prisão cautelar*, long a judicial power cramming the country's jails with its underclass, became for the first time an acceptable instrument for breaking those above it; and sentences in a first court of appeal could no longer be deferred pending confirmation by a higher court, making the route to incarceration much faster. The first two were the weapons that allowed Italian magistrates to lay siege to the Italian political and industrial class in the Tangentopoli scandals of the nineties. The third they never acquired. In Brazil, a further means of extracting confessions from those under pre-emptive lock and key was devised: threats to extend the same treatment to their families. In 2013 wire-taps on a currency exchange counter at a car-wash (Lava Jato) in Brasília led to the arrest of a black-marketeer with a long police record. Held in Curitiba, far to the south, to protect his family this *doleiro* began to reveal the scale of the system of corruption in Petrobras where he had been one of the key intermediaries for the transfer of funds between contractors, directors and politicians, inside and outside the country. Within short order, charges were brought against nine top construction companies in Brazil, and their celebrity CEOs detained; three senior directors of Petrobras were jailed, and investigations opened against over fifty members of Congress and state governors.

The three principal parties involved—they numbered seven in all—were the PMDB, the PP (a sprig of the dictatorship) and the PT. Which banked the most is still unclear. But since few had any illusions about the first two, it was the exposure of the third that mattered politically. The *mensalão* was petty cash by comparison with the enormity of the *petrolão*, and whereas the former had been of no private benefit to members of the PT, it was soon clear that the latter had erased the line between organizational funding and personal enrichment. Among other details, it emerged that Lula's chief of staff José Dirceu, driven from office for his part in the *mensalão*, had thereafter insisted on a cut from the *petrolão* being paid into his own bank accounts. If the bulk of the kick-backs was used to finance the party's campaigns and its apparatus, the continual sloshing about of huge sums of clandestine money could not but corrode those handling it. The sociologist Chico de Oliveira's warning, made well before the *petrolão* came to light, that the PT was descending towards transmogrification into a taxonomically aberrant species of political life, could no longer be dismissed as a mere metaphor.[13]

---

13 See Oliveira, *Crítica à Razão Dualista—O Ornitorrinco*, São Paulo 2003; in English, 'The Duck-Billed Platypus', *New Left Review* 24, November–December 2003, pp. 40–57. In focussing on the PT's policies and its electorate, Singer's work has been criticized by Marcos Nobre for neglecting the party as an organizational machine, and the political system that is the context of its operations: *Imobilismo em movimento*, pp. 181–3. This is what Oliveira's counter-analysis of the PT supplies.

Leading the attack on the *petrolão*, the investigative team in Curitiba became, like the pool in Milan that inspired them, media stars overnight. Youthful, clean-cut and square-jawed, wholesome training at Harvard, judge Sergio Moro and prosecutor Deltan Dallagnol looked straight out of courtroom drama on American television. Of their zeal to root out corruption, and the value of their shock to the business and political elites of the country, there could be no doubt. But as in Italy, aims and methods did not always coincide. Delation for gain, and indefinite incarceration without charge, combine inducement and intimidation: blunt instruments in the search for truth and pursuit of justice, but in Brazil within the law. Leakage of information, or mere suspicion, from investigations still supposedly secret, to the press is not: it is clearly illegal. In Italy, it was regularly used by the Milan Pool, and would be used even more widely by the Pool in Curitiba. From the outset, the leaks looked selective: persistently targeting the PT, and persistently—though not exclusively: titbits were distributed elsewhere—appearing in the most violent battering-ram of media assault on it, the weekly magazine *Veja*, which after weeks of exposés, in the last hours before polls opened in the presidential election of 2014 ran a cover story with the faces of Dilma and Lula looming out a sinister half-light, lurid red and eerie black, over the exclamation 'They Knew!', alerting voters to the criminal master-minds of the *petrolão*.

Did the drip-feed from magistrates to media mean their objectives were the same, the fruit—as the PT already saw it—of an operation in common? The Brazilian judiciary, like its colleagues in the apparatus of prosecutors and federal police, can be assumed to share much the same outlook as the country's middle class, to whose better-off layers they belong, with its typical preferences and prejudices. No worker's party, however emollient, is likely to attract particular sympathy in this milieu. But might the purpose of leaking against the PT be less a tpartisan aversion to it as such than a calculation that there would no better way to dramatize the evils of corruption at large than to pick the PT out for obloquy, as for over a decade the leading political force in the land, and the one about which the media for its own reasons were most eager for revelations? Damaging stories about the PMDB would be too banal for that, and the PSDB could be spared as, at national level, an opposition party with less access to federal coffers, whatever its record at state levels.

The Lava Jato scandal broke in the spring of 2014, and successive arrests and charges kept it in the headlines throughout the presidential contest in the autumn. Dilma's economic U-turn, once elected, may in part have been conducted in the hope of placating neo-liberal opinion sufficiently for the media to moderate its depiction of the PT as a den of thieves. If so, it was in vain. Outflanking even the PSDB in the virulence of its attacks on Dilma, a new Right rocketed to prominence in the mass demonstrations against her of March 2015. In Brazil the slogans of the Right in 1964 were Family, God and Freedom, the banners of a conservatism that hailed the arrival of the military dictatorship. Half a century later, the rallying-cries had changed. Recruited from a younger generation of middle-class activists, a new Right—often proud to call itself such—spoke less of the deity, hardly at all of the family, and reinterpreted liberty. For this layer, a free market was the foundation of every other freedom, the state its hydra-headed enemy. Politics started, not in the institutions of a decaying order, but in the street and squares, where citizens could topple a regime of parasites and robbers. Surfing the mass demonstrations against Dilma, the two leading groups of this radical Right—Vem Pra Rua and Movimento Brasil Livre—have modelled their tactics on the role on the radical Left of Movimento Passe-Livre in sparking the protests of 2013, the second even deliberately echoing its acronym: for MPL read MBL.[14] The organizations are small on both sides of the divide, each relying on mobilization of larger numbers by intensive use of the internet. Brazil has more Facebook addicts than any other country after the United States, and Vem Pra Rua, the MBL and other networks on the Right—Revoltados On-Line (ROL) is another prominent player—have, no doubt predictably, given the class profile of Zuckerberg's following, galvanized them into action with far more success than the Left. To date, the multiplier effects of the new Right have been much greater.

Beyond it lies the ambiguous nebula of new religion. Over a fifth of the population of Brazil are now converts to one variety or another of Evangelical Protestantism.[15] In the pattern of the Unification Church of the Reverend Moon, many of these— certainly the largest—are business rackets milking the faithful for money to erect the financial empires of their founders. The fortune of Edir Macedo, head of the Universal Church of the Kingdom of God, whose huge kitsch Temple of Solomon in the Brás neighbourhood of São Paulo—just across from the scarcely less gross edifice of its rival, the Assembleia de Deus, forming a kind of religious Wall Street—stages melodramatic exorcisms on a big screen before hushed or chanting believers in the dark,

---

14 The best accounts to date of this new force can be found in Luciana Tatagiba, Thiago Trinidade and Ana Claudia Chaves Teixeira, 'Protestos à direita no Brasil (2005-15)', and Sergio Amadeu Silveira, 'Direita nas redes sociais online' in Sebastião Velasco e Cruz, André Kaysel and Gustavo Codas, *Direita, Volver !*, São Paulo 2015, pp. 197-230.

15 For a level-headed survey, see Paul Freston, *Evangelicals and Politics in Asia, Africa and Latin America*, Cambridge 2001, pp. 11-58.

is reckoned at over $1 billion. Along with it comes control of the country's second-largest television chain. Currently hegemonic in the field, Macedo's organization preaches a 'theology of prosperity' promising material success on earth, rather than mere relief in heaven, to those who follow pastors instructing them in the word of the Lord. Unlike American Evangelicals, the Brazilian churches have no marked ideological profiles, other than on such issues as abortion or gay marriage. Macedo supported Cardoso as a bulwark against communism, later fell in behind Lula and since then has created his own political organization. But most of the churches operate much like the undergrowth of Brazilian parties that are vehicles for hire, swapping votes for favours, with the difference that they will back candidates on any number of tickets: the Evangelical caucus in Congress, some 18 per cent of the Lower Chamber, includes deputies from twenty-two parties. Its principal interests lie in securing licenses for their radio and television stations, tax exemption for their businesses and access to real estate for building pharaonic monuments to themselves.

At the same time, if more passively and promiscuously than their counterparts in the US, they form a conservative reservoir for aggressively right-wing leaders in Congress. There, symptomatically, the president of the Evangelical Front is a muscular pastor and former policeman who sits on the benches of the PSDB. There too, elected speaker of the House in February 2015—the most powerful post in Congress, and the third office of state after president and vice-president—was Eduardo Cunha, Evangelical operator from Rio and leader of the PMDB bench. Widely identified as Dilma's most dangerous enemy—she tried to block his election—Cunha's sleek features and imperturbable manner conceal an exceptionally skilled and ruthless politician, a master of the black arts of parliamentary manipulation and management, on whom large numbers of the 'lower clergy' in the House had become dependent for the economics of their arrival there, while others lived in fear of his retribution should they cross him. No sooner had demonstrations in the streets called for Dilma's impeachment than he became the spearhead of the drive in the legislature to oust her, on the pretext that prior to the election she had improperly transferred funds from state banks to federal accounts.

Reaching a crescendo in September, the movement to depose her extended across a broad milieu, in which different forces and figures overlapped in indeterminate ways, the young Turks of MBL and ROL posing for photographs with Cunha, pillars of the law Moro and Dallagnol (another Evangelical) consorting with PSDB politicians and pro-impeachment lobbies, the press pummelling the PT and the Planalto with new denunciations daily. Either Dilma had illegally concealed a deficit in the accounts of the state in order to be re-elected, or she had relied on large injections of corruption to finance her election campaign, or both—in either event, grounds for her speedy ejection from office as an affront to public probity. Eighty per cent of the population, polls showed, already wished her gone.

Into this scene, a bombshell exploded. In mid-October the Swiss authorities notified the attorney-general in Brasília that Cunha held no less than four secret bank accounts in Switzerland—another soon came to light in the US ; one in the name of his wife, another in that of a shell company set up in Singapore, via yet another registered in New Zealand. Total value: $16 million, or thirty-seven times his declared wealth in Brazil. At the disposal of the couple, held in the name of two local companies —defeating satire, one called Jesus.com—was a fleet of nine assorted limousines and SUVs in Rio. Evidence that he had been extracting huge bribes from Petrobras piled up. Even for the most conformist press, this was too much. In Congress, a comedy of reversals ensued. Under the Brazilian Constitution, the Speaker of the House is vested with the sole power to bring a motion for impeachment of the president to the floor. For months the PSDB had been courting Cunha, conferring with him in intimate conclaves on the tactics and timing of the prospective trial. The revelation of his treasure-chest in Switzerland, with evidence immensely more damning than any purported against Dilma, thus came as an acute embarrassment for the party. What was it to do? Cunha still held the keys to impeachment, which if successful would cancel the election of 2014, and ensure Aécio's victory in the re-run. The party therefore said as little as possible about the tidings from Berne, beyond observing that Cunha himself had not yet spoken and must be regarded as innocent until proved otherwise. But at that its backers in the media could not contain themselves: how could the party of morality act as a cover for such blatant criminality? In face of this revolt, the PSDB was forced to back-track and sheepishly announce that it could not after all support the Speaker—a small independent socialist party had by now lodged a case for his removal from Congress—any longer. On seeing the PSDB desert him, Cunha made a swift about-face. Negotiating behind closed doors, he offered to freeze impeachment if the PT would protect him from annulment of his mandate and expulsion from Congress. No sooner said than done. PT ministers, no less shameless than the PSDB, agreed to help him remain in place, provided he made no move against Dilma. This surreal merry-go-round was too much for the PT outside Congress, and the deal had to be dropped. For a time, it looked as if Cunha's position was unsustainable, and the cause of impeachment so damaged by his exposure that it had small chance of passing.

In the background, however, the prime repository of hopes to finish off the PT had not desisted. Since the onset of the crisis, Cardoso had been omnipresent in the media—his image everywhere, adorning a torrent of interviews, articles, speeches, diaries. Long esteemed by press barons and their aides, his renewed prominence was the fruit of a more immediate political calculation on their part, and his. Presented as the elder statesman of the republic, to whose wisdom it owes what stability it ever achieved, editors and journalists have competed to build him up as a thinker of international stature, the voice of sanity and responsibility in the country's dire condition, courtiers in the Anglophone press and academy swelling the chorus of sycophancy.[16] The rationale for this apotheosis is straightforward enough: Cardoso's presidency administered to Brazil its one firm dose of market-friendly management, the medicine it requires more urgently than ever, after the debauches of PT populism. Cardoso himself, who in office lamented that it was 'an immense difficulty' that 'Brazil doesn't like the capitalist system', has no quarrel with that. The PSDB of which he is now the patriarch is social-democratic only in the sense that the PSD of Cavaco Silva in Portugal is so. But he has a more personal stake in the

---

16 In the characteristic tones of the *Economist's* man on Latin America: 'In several meetings with him, I found him a man of polished charm, extraordinarily articulate and an acute analyst of the problems of his country, its region and the world. As president, he had the academic sociologist's sense of the authority of his office, and the manner in which it should and shouldn't be used. Many Brazilians were relieved that at last their country was represented by someone of whom they could feel proud, able to discuss with world leaders fluently in English, French Spanish'—etcetera. Michael Reid, *Brazil: The Troubled Rise of a Global Power*, New Haven 2014, p. 129 et seq.

flood-lights surrounding him. When he left office, his ratings were not much higher than Dilma's today, and for eight years he suffered from comparison with Lula, a far more popular president who repudiated his legacy and changed the country decisively in ways he did not, assuring the PT a mandate twice the length he had enjoyed.

This was a bitter cup to swallow. Could the aura of a thinker make up for loss of prestige as a ruler? Objectively, the second role had—this is normal enough—come at the expense of the first. In pursuit of office Fernando Henrique had sacrificed not only his early convictions, which were Marxist and socialist, but over time his intellectual standards. The banality of his later output—bromides in praise of globalization and anxiety at its side-effects—is dispiriting. On rare occasions, he perhaps glimpses this himself. 'I must admit that, though my intellectual bent is strong, I am basically a *homo politicus*,' he once let slip.[17] But subjectively, vanity—stung by the greater political appeal of a worker with no education—does not allow more cerebral pretensions to be set aside. Clad in the green and gold of the Brazilian Academy, a tropical copy of the pompous French original, sword in its scabbard at his side, he declared a while ago that the sociologist and the president had never diverged in the course of a coherent career and a creative administration, entirely in keeping with each other.

For years, Cardoso had reason to complain that in opposition the PSDB itself had been insufficiently loyal to the memory of its outstanding leader, avoiding any vigorous defence of his modernization of Brazil, and its courageous privatizations. Now, however, the crisis of *lulopetismo*—his regular disdainful

---

17 See Cardoso's collection *A Miséria da política: Crônicas do lulopetismo e outros escritos*, Rio de Janeiro 2015, p. 66.

term—showed how right he had been all along. If there was anything good under PT rule, it was an inheritance from him. If there was so much more that was disastrously bad, it was just what he had always warned against. The time had come to uphold the banners of 1994 and 1998 with pride again, and put an end to the misrule of the PT.[18] Though he himself was not yet calling for it, impeachment was a perfectly proper process, if grounds for it were established. Even if they were not, Dilma could scarcely recover politically. But—here Cardoso's calculations differed from the younger generation of PSDB politicians in Congress, eager to snatch power from her overnight—it was best to wait for the findings of the judiciary, which could be counted on to see political justice done.

That confidence, born of close connexions with senior judges, was unlikely to prove misplaced. Due to preside over the case against Dilma on the Supreme Electoral Tribunal was Gilmar Mendes, a crony Cardoso had appointed to the country's Supreme Court, where he still sits, who has never concealed his dislike of the PT. But Dilma was lesser prey. For Cardoso, the crucial target for destruction was Lula, not simply for reasons of revenge, however much this might be savoured in private, but because there was no telling, given his past popularity, whether he might capable of a political comeback in 2018—when, if Dilma survived till then, the PSDB should otherwise be able to count on steering the country back to a responsible modernity once more. No sooner were Cardoso's hints dropped than a steady

18 For a valiant attempt to cast this project in a renewed social-democratic light, while ascribing the PSDB's later discomfort with Cardoso's legacy in part to the technocratic style of his government, in which the party itself was effaced, see Sergio Fausto, 'Crise do PT dá oportunidade ao PSDB para reencontrar sua identidade', Folha, 2 August 2015. Fausto is the director of Cardoso's foundation, the FHC Institute.

drip of leaks from the Lava Jato pool started to appear in the press implicating Lula in dubious financial transactions of a personal kind: trips abroad in corporate jets, speeches remunerated by construction companies, deposits on costly beach-side quarters, refurbishments of a rural retreat, not to mention obscure earnings by one of his sons. Next came the arrest of a millionaire rancher friend, charged with passing the kickback on a Petrobras contract to the treasury of the PT. To all appearances, the net was closing in on him.

Promptly, in the first week of March, a large squad of federal police arrived at Lula's door at six o'clock in the morning and took him into custody for interrogation at São Paulo airport. The press, informed beforehand, was waiting outside to swarm forward with its cameras, for maximum publicity. The pretext for the show was that if simply asked for testimony, he might have absconded. The following week the largest demonstrations in Brazil since the dictatorship—according to the police, 3.7 million strong—clamoured for justice against him, and impeachment for Dilma. Three days later, Dilma appointed him *Chefe da Casa Civil*—equivalent to prime minister—in her government. As a minister, Lula would enjoy immunity from charges at Moro's level in Curitiba, becoming subject, like all other members of the Government and of Congress, only to the Supreme Court. Moro wasted no time. That afternoon he published wire-taps of a phone conversation between Dilma and Lula in which she told him that she could send him the paper-work requiring his signature for the appointment 'if necessary'. Her phrasing was ambiguous. But the media uproar was deafening: here, caught red-handed, was a manoeuvre to thwart justice by whisking Lula out of reach of the law. Within twenty-four hours, the nomination was blocked by a judge in Brasília—one who, it soon emerged, had posted images of himself prancing on pro-impeachment demonstrations, clad in a PSDB t-shirt. But he was swiftly backed by Mendes, and within a fortnight the PMDB announced it was abandoning the government, in which it held the vice-presidency and six ministries, paving the way for a rapid eviction of Dilma by Congress.

In this dramatic escalation of the political crisis of the country, the central player was the judiciary. The notion that Moro's operation was acting impartially in Curitiba, initially defensible, stood ruined with the gratuitous, media-orchestrated theatre of his dawn raid on Lula's home, followed by a public message saluting the demonstrations demanding Dilma's impeachment. 'Brazil is in the streets', he announced, 'I am touched'. In then publishing wire-taps of a phone call between Lula and Dilma, hours after the bugging was supposed to have been halted, he broke the law twice over—violating the seal covering such interceptions, even when they were permitted, not to speak of the confidentiality supposedly protecting communications of the head of state. So patent were these illegalities that they brought down a lukewarm rebuke from the judge on the Supreme Court to whom he is formally responsible, but no sanction. Though 'inappropriate', as his superior mildly put it, his action had achieved its desired effect.

In most contemporary democracies, the separation of powers is a polite fiction, supreme courts in general—the one in Washington is an intermittent exception—bending to the will of the governments of the day. The contortions of the German Constitutional Court—often cited as a luminous example of judicial independence—in upholding violations both of the country's *Grundgesetz* and the Treaty of Maastricht at the behest of successive regimes in Berlin, can be taken as the norm. In

Brazil, the politicization of the higher judiciary is a long tradition. The Ubuesque figure of Gilmar Mendes is perhaps an extreme case, if a revealing one. As president, Cardoso shielded his friend from charges at law by giving him ministerial status—Mendes now excoriates Dilma for doing this with Lula—before elevating him to the Supreme Court. There, to avoid unwelcome attention, Cardoso would slip into the building by the underground garage to confer with him. Too blatant a partisan of the PSDB—*tucano demais*—for even Eliane Cantanhêde, an admiring interviewer of the right, Mendes could be seen lunching convivially with prominent leaders of the party after acquitting them of misdeeds, and did not hesitate to employ public funds to enroll subordinates in a private law school he ran for profit, while sitting as a judge in the highest tribunal of the nation. His fulminations against the PT are legion.

Sergio Moro, a generation younger, is of another stamp. The United States, where he was trained and often visits, is his land of reference. A hard-working provincial, he owes nothing to patronage or commerce. But early on—he was just past thirty— he displayed his indifference to basic principles of law or rules of evidence, in an article extolling the example of the Italian magistrates of the nineties, *Considerações sobre a Operação Mani Pulite*, in terms that anticipated his procedures a decade later. Making no attempt to research the extensive literature on Tangentopoli, he contented himself with two encomia of the Milan Pool available to American readers, citing these without a hint of critical reflection, and took as gospel the claims of a *pentito* mafia boss living on a stipend from the state, despite their rejection in court. Presumption of innocence could not be regarded as an 'absolute', he declared: it was merely a 'pragmatic instrument', that could be over-ridden at the will of the magistrate. Leaks to the media he celebrated as a form of 'pressure' on defendants, where 'legitimate aims cannot be achieved by other methods'.

The danger of a judiciary actuated in this spirit is the same in Brazil as it was in Italy: an absolutely necessary campaign against corruption becomes so infected with disregard for due process, and unscrupulous collusion with the media, that rather than instilling any new ethic of legality, it ends by confirming long-standing social disrespect for the law. Berlusconi and his heir are the living proof of that. The scene in Brazil differs from the situation in Italy, however, in two respects. No Berlusconi or Renzi is in sight. Moro, whose celebrity now exceeds that of any of his Italian role-models, will no doubt be solicited to fill the political vacuum, should Lava Jato make a clean sweep of the old order. But the mediocre destiny of Di Pietro, the most popular of the Milan magistrates, stands as a warning to Moro, anyway more genuinely puritan in outlook, against the temptation to enter politics. The space for a meteoric ascent is also likely to be less, because of a further critical difference between the two crusades against corruption. The assault on Tangentopoli struck at the traditional rulers of the country, Christian Democracy and the Socialist Party, who had been in power together for thirty years; whereas Lava Jato has taken political aim, not at the country's traditional rulers, whom it has—hitherto—largely spared, but at the upstarts who displaced them. It looks much more one-sided, and so divisive.

The division has been enormously accentuated by a second difference between the Italy of the early nineties and Brazil today. When Tangentopoli hit the political system, the Italian media formed a heterogeneous landscape. Independent newspapers tended to back the judiciary in Milan across the board. The press conglomerate of the Olivetti boss De Benedetti, where most of the leaks appeared, trumpeted the charges against Christian Democrats and Socialists, while keeping as quiet as possible about others implicating its owner. Berlusconi's television and press empire let fly at the magistrates. The result was that, as time went on, there was far more questioning of the actions of the different rungs of the judiciary—many very courageous, others very dubious—than in Brazil. There, the media have been monolithically partisan in their hostility to the PT, and uncritical of the strategy of leaks and pressures from Curitiba, of which they have acted as the boom-box. Brazil boasts some of the finest columnists in the world, whose writing has analysed the current crisis at a literary and intellectual level far above the scrublands of the *Guardian* or *New York Times*. But such voices are vastly outnumbered by a forest of conformists echoing the outlook of owners and editors.

To compare the coverage in the media of any leak or revelation damaging the PT with its treatment of information or rumour affecting the opposition is to measure the extent of its double standards. As Lava Jato was unfolding, there flickered for a moment alongside it a poignant example. In 1989, in one of the most famous turning-points of modern Brazilian history, Lula— then still a dangerous radical in the eyes of the establishment —was within reach of victory in his initial run for the presidency, when a few days before the decisive vote, a former girlfriend appeared on a television broadcast for his opponent Collor, paid by Collor's brother to do so, accusing him of having wanted to abort the pregnancy with a child by him. The sensation, magnified to the limit in the media, clinched his defeat on polling day. Two years later Cardoso—then a prominent PSDB Senator, already tipped as a future presidential candidate—was known in political circles to have a mistress working for the very television chain, TV Globo, that had ruined Lula. When she gave birth to a child, she was spirited out of the country *en poste* to Portugal. By mid 1994, after serving as finance minister, Cardoso was running for the presidency, and his mistress's work became increasingly nominal, though Globo continued to cover her salary. Once he was elected, his right-hand man, the younger Magalhães, instructed her not to return to Brazil for fear of compromising his re-election. When Globo cut her salary, a fictional job was found for her, supposedly doing market research in Europe for a duty-free chain granted monopoly rights in Brazilian airports by Cardoso. Through this firm, her own telling would imply, he had laundered $100,000 to her—child support or hush money?—via one of its accounts in the Cayman Islands. The story broke this February, in the midst of the media tornado around Lula's housing arrangements. The media made sure it received the least possible coverage. The firm is now under investigation for a criminal transaction. Cardoso protests his innocence. No one expects him to suffer any inconvenience.

Could the same be said of the opposition at large? Moro released his incendiary wiretaps on March 16. A week later, police in São Paulo raided the home of one of the executives of Odebrecht, the largest construction firm in Latin America, whose head had just been sentenced to nineteen years in prison for bribery. There they found a set of tables listing 316 leading politicians with amounts of cash against their names. Included were top figures in the PSDB, PMDB and many other parties— a panorama of Brazil's political class. Objectively speaking, its publication was a louder thunder-clap than an exchange between Dilma and Lula. But a less convenient one. From Curitiba, Moro took immediate action in the opposite direction, ordering the tables be put under seal to prevent further speculation about them. Still, an alarm had gone off: Lava Jato could get out of hand. If Dilma was to be toppled, it was critical it be done before the Odebrecht tables could threaten her accusers. Within a few days, the PMDB announced that it was abandoning the government, and the countdown to a vote on impeachment had begun. The three-fifths majority of the Lower Chamber which had looked too high a bar at the beginning of the year was now within reach.

As the pressure of the right on Dilma escalated, it became increasingly clear that only popular mobilization could stop her ouster. But that was fettered by the legacy of PT rule. The party was in a poor position to call on its beneficiaries to defend it, for at least three reasons. The first is simply that if corruption lost it middle-class sympathy it once enjoyed, austerity alienated the much larger lower-class base it acquired. The demonstrations it managed to convoke against impeachment were much less imposing than those calling for it. Marchers were mustered mainly from public sector workers and unions: the poor conspicuous by their absence. Its rural bailiwicks in the North-East are anyway socially dispersed, as the big cities of the Centre-South that are the strongholds of the new right are not. Then there was the inevitable demoralization as successive scandals have engulfed the party, a diffuse sense of guilt, however suppressed, weakening any fighting spirit.

Lastly, and most fundamentally, by the time Lula won power, the party had become essentially an electoral machine : financed overwhelmingly by corporate donations rather than—as at the beginning—by members' dues, contenting itself with passive adhesion to the name of its leader, lacking any will to foster collective action among its voters. The active mobilization that brought into it being in the manufacturing centres of Brazil became a distant memory as the party spread to zones of the country and layers of the population untouched by industry, with deep-rooted traditions of submission to authority and fear of disorder. This was a political culture Lula understood, and did not seriously attempt to unsettle. In his vision of things, the potential cost of doing so was too high. To help the masses he sought harmony with the elites, for whom any vigorous polarization was taboo. In 2002 he finally won the presidency, at his fourth attempt, on a slogan of 'peace and love'. In 2016, faced with political lynching, he was still uttering the same two words to crowds expecting something more combative.

Such discordance between attack and response is the mark of a pattern that, since the turn of the century, has distinguished Brazilian politics within Latin America. It is not the only country that has seen class conflict escalating in a crisis. But nowhere else has this been so one-sided. Even when Lula was at the peak of his prestige as a ruler, there was always an asymmetry between the moderate and accommodating policies of the PT, and the hostility of an *enragé* middle class and media against it. Over the past eighteen months, the expressions of that unilateral abhorrence have become ever more violent. A municipal councillor of the PMDB in the interior of São Paulo could publicly call for Lula to be killed like a viper crushed underfoot. In Rio Grande do Sul, to the south, a pediatrician refused to attend to a one-year-old child because the mother was a *petista*, and was upheld by the Regional Council of Medicine and Association of Doctors for doing so. The judge on the Supreme Court responsible for issuing a mild pro forma reproof to Moro was rewarded with banners outside his apartment denouncing him as a 'Traitor' and 'Stooge of the PT', while demonstrators struck up their signature song, 'Capitalism Is Here to Stay'. As D-day for impeachment approached, zealots were supplied with the addresses of deputies thought to be recalcitrant, fanning out across the country to intimidate them by camping outside their homes. Meticulously, the stock market kept pace: soaring when Lula was taken into custody, dropping when he was made chief of staff, rising again when his appointment was blocked. In advance, respectable opinion issued a *placet* to the farce of a Congress packed with thieves, Cunha at their head, solemnly deposing a president for budgetary irregularity.

On April 17, the Chamber of Deputies, over half of whose members face criminal investigations of one kind or another, duly voted to impeach the president. Orchestrated by Cunha, the most notorious political crook in the country, deputy after deputy, paying no attention to the charges nominally held against her, rose to invoke God and the Family as they cast their votes in favour of driving her from office. From Rio, former army parachutist Jair Bolsonaro, exulting in a victory to match that of 1964, when the military saved the country from communism, dedicated his ballot to the memory of Colonel Carlos Brilhante Ustra, torturer of the dictatorship that followed. He had reason to celebrate. Without the thirty-seven votes supplied by his party and the current incarnation of the PFL, the launch to impeachment would have failed. The next day, rejoicing at the outcome, Cardoso enthused that this degrading spectacle was a 'lovely, positive demonstration of democracy'.[19] *Bonita e positiva*, no less.

Three weeks later, the Senate voted to evict Dilma from office for six months, pending a trial whose outcome is a foregone conclusion, and to install as interim ruler of the country her vice-president, the sepulchral PMDB veteran Michel Temer— famously compared to 'a major-domo in a horror film'—who had deserted her well beforehand, preparing the way some

---

19 *Folha*, 18 April 2016.

months earlier by commissioning an economic programme to make clear that the nation would be in safe hands if he took over. The package was a conventional stabilization plan, comprising privatizations, pension reform and abolition of constitutionally mandated expenditures on health and education, assorted with promises of care for the least fortunate. With a three-fifths majority behind him, Temer has had no trouble forming a coalition government bringing together the PMDB, PP, PSDB, and a motley array of lesser parties. Since such a combine can pass legislation, as Dilma could not, and business confidence will return, his regime should be able to improve the economic indicators that matter to financial markets, whatever the costs to the poor. But given an adverse global conjuncture, and the stubbornly low rate of investment that has persisted in Brazil since the end of dictatorship, it is difficult to see much relief for the country ahead.

Politically, too, stability is scarcely guaranteed. One obvious question is whether the shock of impeachment will so cow the forces that have supported Dilma that little fight is left in them, or on the contrary provoke fiercer resistance to the country's establishment than in the past. Nor is all likely to be easy in the ranks of the victors. One awkwardness further down the road is that still pending before the Supreme Electoral Tribunal is a joint charge against Dilma and Temer—launched by the PSDB when it hoped to scoop the pool by forcing new elections quickly—that their ticket in 2014 violated campaign regulations, which if upheld would cashier both of them. The suit cannot be withdrawn, but since Mendes becomes president of the Tribunal in May, Brazilian justice can probably be trusted to finesse the difficulty. A larger question-mark, of course, is what subsequent impact Lava Jato could have on the impeachers themselves. His task as architect of impeachment performed, Cunha was promptly side-lined by a judge on the Supreme Court to cleanse the image of the new regime, in a blatantly political—indeed, unconstitutional —decision. But at least five members of Temer's cabinet, including his PMDB colleague in charge of Planning and his PSDB ally in the Foreign Ministry, are implicated in ongoing investigations of corruption. The drama of impeachment served to deflect public attention from the tables of Odebrecht. But can they be erased from memory thereafter? In their columns a whole political class is at stake. Could Brazilian justice finesse its difficulties too—in the interests, it goes without saying, of national reconciliation?

That the Workers' Party has rejoined, by a mutation of its own, the deformed ranks of the rest of Brazilian political fauna—the PMDB, PSDB, PP and their ilk—is past denial. By now two presidents of the party, two treasurers, a president and vice-president of the lower house and the leader of the party in the upper house, have all found themselves in jail, sunk in a quicksand of corruption that knows no political borders. Emblematically, the latest of its notables to fall, and the most voluble in delation, Senator Delcídio do Amaral, is a transfuge from the PSDB, where he was a stalwart of Cardoso's party in the machinery of Petrobras. Half or more of the entire Congress is on the payroll of construction companies, whose donations finance their election. The degradation of the political system has become so patent that last autumn the Supreme Court—itself far from any Areopagus of impartial integrity—finally ruled that corporate funding of electoral campaigns is unconstitutional, banning company donations outright. Congress immediately reacted with constitutional amendments to reinstate them, whose issue is in baulk. But if confirmed, and not circumvented, the decision will amount to a revolution in the workings of Brazilian democracy: the one unequivocally positive outcome of the crisis to date. The Workers' Party believed, after a time, that it could use the established order in Brazil to benefit the poor, without harm to the rich, indeed with their help. It did benefit the poor, as it set out to do. But once it accepted the price of entry into a diseased political system, the door closed behind it. The party itself withered, becoming an enclave in the state, without self-awareness or strategic direction, so blind that it ostracized its best thinker for a mess of spin-doctors and pollsters, so insensible it took lucre, wherever it came from, as the condition of power. Its achievements will remain. Whether it will itself do so is an open question. In South America, a cycle is coming to an end. For a decade and a half, relieved of the attentions of the US, buoyed by the commodities boom, and drawing on deep reserves of popular tradition, the continent was the only part of the world where rebellious social movements coexisted with heterodox governments. In the wake of 2008, there are now plenty of the former elsewhere. But none so far of the latter. A global exception is closing, with no relay yet in sight.

5

BOLSONARO

January 2019

The teratology of the contemporary political imagination—plentiful enough: Trump, Le Pen, Salvini, Orbán, Kaczynski, ogres galore—has acquired a new monster. Rising above the ruck, the president-elect of Brazil has extolled his country's most notorious torturer; declared that its military dictatorship should have shot 30,000 opponents; told a congresswoman she was too ugly to merit raping; announced he would rather a son of his were killed in a car accident than gay; declared open season on the Amazon rainforest; and, not least, on the day after his election, promised followers to rid the land of red riff-raff. For his incoming minister of justice, Sergio Moro—no ordinary magistrate: saluted worldwide as an epitome of judicial independence and integrity—Jair Bolsonaro is a 'moderate'.

To all appearances, the verdict of the polls last October was unambiguous: after governing the country for fourteen years, the Worker's Party led by Lula and Dilma has been comprehensively repudiated, and its very survival may now be in doubt. Incarcerated by Moro, the most popular ruler in Brazilian history awaits further sentences of imprisonment. His successor, evicted from office midway through her second term, is a virtual outcast, reduced to a humiliating fourth place in a local contest for a seat in the Senate. How has this reversal come about? To what extent was it contingent, or at some point a foregone conclusion? What explains the radicalism of the upshot? By comparison with the scale of the upheaval through which Brazil has lived in the last five years, and the gravity of its possible outcome, the histrionics over Brexit in this country and the conniptions over Trump in America are close to much ado about nothing.

Brazilian politics are Italianate in character: intricate and serpentine. But there is little grasping what has happened to the country without some understanding of them. When Lula left office in 2010—presidents in Brazil are limited to two successive terms, though not barred from subsequent re-election—the economy posted 7.5 per cent growth, poverty had been cut in half, new universities had multiplied, inflation was low, the budget and current account were in surplus, and his approval ratings over 80 per cent. To succeed him, he picked his chief of staff, Dilma Rousseff, in the sixties a fighter in the underground against the military dictatorship of the period, who had never held or run for electoral office before. With Lula at her side, she coasted to victory with a 56 per cent majority, becoming the first woman to win the country's presidency. Initially better received by a middle class that detested Lula, for two years she enjoyed quite widespread esteem, for a show of calm and competence. But her inheritance was less rosy than it seemed. Economically, high commodity prices had underlain the boom under Lula, without altering Brazil's historically low rates of investment and productivity growth. Virtually as soon as Dilma took office in 2011, they started to fall, bringing growth abruptly down to 1.9 per cent by 2012. In 2013 the Federal Reserve announced it would stop buying bonds, setting off the so-called taper tantrum in capital markets and drawing foreign finance out of the country. The balance of payments deteriorated. Inflation picked up. The years of buoyant prosperity were over.

Politically, moreover, a mortgage lay on PT government from the start. After the re-democratization of the country in the late eighties, three parties loomed largest: on the centre-right, the fig-leaf 'social-democratic' PSDB, home of big business and the middle class; in the middle, the theoretically 'democratic' PMDB, a sprawling network of clientelism in rural and small-town back-waters, feathering local nests with federal or provincial largesse; on the left, the PT, the only party that was more than a collec-tion of regional notables and their underlings. Alongside this trio, however, in Brazil's open-list proportional representation in very large constituencies, a plethora of smaller parties of no ideological orientation, contraptions for extracting public funds and favours for their leaders, proliferated. In these conditions, no president has ever led a party with more than a quarter of the seats in a Congress through which all significant legislation must pass, making coalitions a condition of government, and distribution of lucrative prebends a condition of coalitions.

For twenty years, the presidency was held by only two parties, the PSDB and the PT. The former, committed to delivering what it called a salutary 'shock of capitalism' to the country, had little difficulty finding allies in the traditional oligarchies of the North-East, and the eternal predators of the PMDB. These were natural allies for a liberal-conservative regime. When Lula came to power, the PT did not want to depend on them. Instead it set out to build a majority in Congress from the morass of smaller parties, each more venal than the next. To avoid them taking too many Ministries, the customary prize for support, it doled out monthly cash payments to them under the counter. When this system, the so-called *mensalão*, was exposed in 2005, it looked for a time as if it might bring down the government. But Lula remained popular among the poor, and by shedding key aides and switching to a more conventional reliance on the PMDB to secure majorities Congress, survived the uproar and in due course was triumphantly re-elected. By his second term the PMDB was a stable brace of his administration, enjoying in exchange a swathe of satisfactory nominations in the machinery of government, central and local, from Ministries on down-wards. When the term came to an end, its Speaker in the Lower Chamber, Michel Temer, a personification of the procedures and outlook of the party, was chosen by Lula to be vice-president under Dilma, yoking a veteran of back-room carve-up and corridor intrigue to a political tyro.

The economic bequests detonated first. By 2013, the middle classes had soured on the government, and rising prices were causing popular tension in the big cities. Lula had pumped money—increased minimum wages, cheaper credits, cash transfers—for the poor into private consumption, rather public services, most of which remained dire. In the winter, higher fares for public transport ignited protests led by young left-wing activists in São Paulo. Police crack-downs amplified them into massive street demonstrations throughout Brazil. With increasing right-wing participation and backing from the country's powerful establishment media, these swiftly became a free-for-all against politicians in general and the PT in particular. In a fortnight Dilma's approval ratings dropped from 57 to 30 per cent. Combining spending cuts and further, inexpensive welfare measures, she recovered ground over the next months. But in the summer of 2014, buried political mines from the past began to explode. Federal police taps on money-laundering operations in a Brasilia car-wash—*lava jato*—revealed widespread corruption in the giant state oil company Petrobras, which at the time boasted one of the largest stock valuations in the world. A stream of leaks from the investigation into it, blared crescendo by the media, indicated connexions to the PT going back to Lula's time. These resonated in an already highly charged atmosphere, formed by the public trial in late 2012—seven years after they were accused—of the party's leading actors in the *mensalão* affair.

So when Dilma ran for re-election in 2014, she faced a far more aggressive opposition than in 2010. As then, it was the PSDB candidate who reached the second round of the presidential contest against her. This time it was a sprig of the traditional political class of Minas Gerais, Aécio Neves, playboy grandson of the politician who would have been the first post-military president in 1985, had he not died before his inauguration. Confident of victory, attacking Dilma ferociously for incompetence, profligacy and suspected delinquency, he came close to beating her. After a combative but clumsy campaign, in which she performed poorly in debate, Dilma achieved a narrow majority on a pledge never to accept the austerity she accused her opponent of planning to inflict on the population. Before even taking office, she was in difficulties. Perhaps thinking to repeat Lula's opening gambit on first becoming president, when he began with strict economic orthodoxy to reassure the markets, expanding social expenditure only after he had consolidated public finances, she picked a Chicago-trained bank executive for minister of finance to signal a new frugality, and betrayed her campaign promises with a conventional retrenchment hitting popular incomes. Having alienated her left, she then antagonized her right by attempting to prevent the PMDB from claiming the powerful position, once occupied by Temer, of Speaker of the House, on whose cooperation passage of legislation generally depended—only to be roundly defeated by the party's victorious candidate Eduardo Cunha, a byword for ruthless cunning and lack of scruple. The PT, which had won just 13 per cent of the vote for Congress, was now extremely vulnerable in the legislature.

The PSDB, meanwhile, had not taken its defeat for the presidency lying down. Furious at being baulked of a triumph on which he had counted, Aécio lodged charges of illegal expenditure against the winning ticket with the Supreme Electoral Tribunal, hoping to get the result annulled and a new poll instituted, in which—given popular disillusion with Dilma's economic course—he could this time be sure of success. But the PSDB, a conglomerate of well-heeled notables in which others had their own ambitions, was not of one mind behind him. The party's unsuccessful candidate for the presidency in 2002 and 2010, José Serra, now a Senator for São Paulo, saw a different path to the eviction of Dilma, one that could broaden support for her ouster and play into his own hands. The drawback of Aécio's route was that it threatened Temer as well as Dilma. It therefore had small appeal for the PMDB. Serra was close to Temer; in São Paulo politics, they had long been associates. Better then to launch impeachment proceedings against Dilma in Congress, where Cunha could be expected to give them a favourable hearing. Success would automatically make Temer president and give Serra—become his quasi-prime minister—the ideal launching pad to succeed him, pipping Aécio for the presidency.

Temer understandably warmed to this scheme, and

surreptitiously the two coordinated moves to realize it. Behind them lay, yet more discreetly, the PSDB's elder statesman Cardoso, an intimate friend and counsellor of Serra, who had never liked Aécio. It only remained to work out a pretext for impeachment. Consensus was reached on a technicality: Dilma had broken the law by deferring payments on public accounts to make them look better for electoral purposes. That this had been a long-standing practice, common to previous governments, scarcely mattered. For by mid 2015, the political landscape had been transformed by an earthquake engulfing the manoeuvres in Brasília.

From the start, the Lava Jato investigations had fallen under the jurisdiction of the home state of the first mid-level culprit to be caught, the *doleiro* (black market money-changer) Alberto Youssef: the atypically middle-class provincial society of Paraná, in the south of Brazil. There Moro, a native son who had cut his teeth as an assistant in the *mensalão* trial, was the presiding judge in its capital Curitiba. His operational model, as he made clear in an article published a decade before Lava Jato was launched, would be the Mani Pulite prosecutions of corruption in Italy by a pool of magistrates in Milan, which had destroyed the governing parties in the early nineties, bringing the First Republic to an end. Moro singled out two features of their campaign for praise: the use of preventive detention to secure delations, and calibrated leaks to the press about ongoing investigations, to goad public opinion into putting pressure on targets and courts. Dramatization in the media mattered more than the presumption of innocence, which Moro explained was subject to pragmatic considerations.[1] In charge of Lava-Jato, he proved an exceptional

---

1 'Considerações sobre a operação Mani Pulite', *Revista CEJ*, No 26, July–September 2004, pp. 56–62.

impresario. Successive operations—raids, round-ups, hand-cuffs, confessions—were given maximum publicity, with tip-offs to press and television, each carefully assigned a number (to date there have been fifty-seven, resulting in over a thousand years of jail sentences), and typically a code name calculated for operatic effect from the cinematic, classical or biblical imaginary: *Bidone, Dolce Vita, Casablanca, Nessun Dorma, Erga Omnes, Aletheia, Last Judgment, Déjà Vu, Omertà, Abyss,* etcetera. Italians pride themselves on a national flair for the spectacle: Moro's management left his Milanese mentors looking flat-footed.

For a year, the Lava Jato operations focussed above all on former directors of Petrobras, charged with receiving and dispensing huge bribes. Then in the spring of 2015, they brought down the first prominent cadre of the PT, its treasurer João Vaccari Neto, arrested in April. A few weeks later the heads of the two largest construction firms in the country, Odebrecht and Andrade Gutierrez, each a continental conglomerate operating across Latin America, were hauled away. By now, demonstrations in support of Moro, clamouring for punishment of the PT and removal of Dilma were building up and putting Congress under siege, where Cunha—still formally part of the ruling coalition—edged towards clearing the docket for impeachment. Isolated and weakened, Dilma accepted her PT ministers' advice that Lula must be called in, as the only person skilled enough in the ways of a Congress she had been unable to master, to try and save the situation. He swiftly set about mending fences with the PMDB. As he did so, it suddenly and spectacularly came out that Cunha had millions of dollars in secret bank accounts in Switzerland. Whereupon, himself now threatened with destruction by Lava Jato, Cunha offered a pact of mutual protection: he would block proceedings against Dilma if the government blocked proceedings against him. Lula urged acceptance of the deal, and at summit level in Brasília an understanding was reached. But the national leadership of the PT, based in São Paulo, fearing news of this arrangement could only confirm public perception of the party as utterly corrupt, instructed its deputies to vote for action against Cunha. In retaliation, he immediately cleared the PSDB-crafted charges against Dilma for deliberation in Congress.

Moro, meanwhile, was preparing his *coup de grâce*. In the first week of March 2016, Operation *Aletheia* seized Lula in the early hours of the morning, taking him in for interrogation, as camera-crews of press and television, tipped off in advance, blazed around him in the darkness. He was now under formal Lava Jato investigation. Further sensation followed. A phone call from Dilma to Lula to discuss the modalities of appointing him as her chief of staff in Brasília was wire-tapped by Moro, and instantly released to the press. Since politicians of ministerial rank, as well as members of Congress, enjoy immunity from prosecution unless authorized by the Supreme Court, there was uproar. This was simply a way of shielding Lula from arrest. The appointment was struck down by two judges in Brasília, the first a public vociferator against the PT on Facebook, the second the well-known placeman of the PSDB on the Supreme Court.

Street pressure for impeachment was by now enormous: across Brazil, 3.6 million demonstrators clamouring for Dilma's eviction in mid-March. Yet it was still far from clear that the necessary two-thirds majority for impeachment could be reached in Congress. Within short order, however, a Lava Jato raid uncovered the notebooks Odebrecht had kept, logging ciphered payments to what was widely rumoured to be some two hundred Brazilian politicians, of virtually all parties. At this, the sirens went off in the political class. Within days Romero Jucá, former leader of government in the Senate, another top power-broker in the PMDB, was taped telling a colleague that 'this bleeding has got to be stopped'. Since 'the guys in the Supreme Court' had told him this was impossible so long as Dilma was in place and the media in full cry after her, he went on, she had to be replaced by Temer right away, and a national government formed, backed by the Supreme Court and the army—he had been talking with generals. Only in this way could Lava Jato be halted before it got to themselves.[2] Within a fortnight the House voted for Dilma's impeachment, Cunha presiding. Having served his purpose, Moro could then pick off Cunha. The Supreme Court ordered Congress to dismiss him as Speaker, in due course he was expelled from the House, and ended in prison. After a required interval, the Senate condemned Dilma on the indictment passed by the House, and Temer took over the presidency. In April 2018, Lula was arrested on a charge of corruption in the prospective acquisition of a sea-front apartment, of which he had never become owner. Tried in Curitiba that summer, he was sentenced to nine years in jail; when he appealed, they were increased to twelve. Its first president behind bars, its second driven igno-miniously from office, its popular standing at an all-time low, the wreckage of the PT looked all but complete.

That this was not effectually so, reaction to Lula's incarcera-tion began to show. Enemies in the PSDB had counted on him going into exile rather than prison, flight to safety sealing his fall from grace. Taken aback by his stoical acceptance of jail, they failed to reckon with the sympathy his imprisonment might arouse. Within a few months, polls showed he was once again the most popular leader in the country, and ahead, even disqualified

---

2   'Em diálogos gravados, Jucá fala em pacto para deter o avanço da Lava Jato', *Folha*, 23 May 2016.

as a felon, of all others in the 2018 contest for the presidency in 2018. Lula's personal appeal, however, was one thing, the future of the PT another. The party had suffered a debacle without precedent in Brazilian history. What kind of reckoning was required to redress it? In its years of power, it had done little to foster a culture of self-critical analysis or reflection on where it, or the country, was going: no newspaper, no journals, no radio or TV stations. Intellectuals had been useful as a bridge to public visibility in the early days. Once in office, though many—perhaps most—continued to support it, the party essentially ignored them, in a myopic philistinism for which all that mattered was electoral calculation.

Undeserved and unappreciated though he was, the party possessed one political thinker of the first rank. Son of an Austrian Jewish immigrant who became a leading Left economist in Brazil, André Singer was a founder member of the PT in São Paulo in 1980. He began as journalist, rising to a senior position in the less conservative of the city's two newspapers, the *Folha*, before becoming press secretary and presidential spokesman for Lula during his first term in Brasília, at the end of which he resigned to take up an academic career as a political scientist. In 2012, he produced the first serious study of the trajectory of its rule and of its social support under Lula, *Os sentidos do Lulismo*. Though written with respectful admiration for what had been achieved, it was too calmly clear-eyed about the nature and causes of the 'weak reformism' it represented to find favour with the party, and had little echo within it. Last summer he published a sequel, *O Lulismo em crise. Um quebra-cabeça do período Dilma (2011–2016)* [Lulism in Crisis: A Conundrum of the Dilma Period], which—even if there is little sign of it yet—may be hoped will meet less silence. From time to time, in different countries, books are compared to Marx's *Eighteenth Brumaire*, but as a dazzling synthesis of class analysis, political narrative and historical imagination, none has ever really approached it till this tour de force from Brazil. Singer's tone, cool and sober, passion contained rather than expressed, is quite different from the blaze of Marx's caustic irony and metaphoric intensity, and the events at issue have been, so far at any rate, less blood-soaked and precipitous. But the kind of intelligence at work, and its scope, are kin.

The puzzle Singer sets out to resolve is why, from the peak of its success under Lula, the formula of power he constructed disintegrated into such wholesale disaster. His opening argument is that it was no familiar case of entropy in office. Dilma was not just a maladroit imitation of her predecessor, bungling in pursuit of the same policies. She had objectives of her own that differed from his. These Singer characterizes as a combination of 'developmentalism' and 'republicanism'. The first, he argues, was a bid to accelerate growth by way of a more ambitious use of the tools available to the national state: control of interest rates, public lending, fiscal incentives, import duties, social expenditures—in sum a significantly more interventionist set of economic policies than the PT had attempted hitherto. By the second, he means republicanism in the classic sense, as reconstructed by Pocock: that is, the seventeenth- and eighteenth-century belief that corruption was a perpetual danger to the integrity of the state and the safety of citizens, vigilance against which was a condition of liberty. Where Lula's had been a weak reformism, Dilma's project aimed at a stronger version.

Its effect, however, was—Singer's second argument—to knock away two critical struts of Lula's system, his entente with financial capital and his pact with clientelism. With the aim of stimulating investment, Dilma's 'new economic matrix' sought to favour domestic industry—which had long complained of Brazil's sky-high interest rates, over-valued currency, weak protection of local manufactures, and costly energy inputs—in the belief that its underlying interests divided it from banks, securities firms and pension funds that benefited from these. But in Brazil the different sectors of capital were too closely intertwined for such a strategy of separation to work. Denounced in the media as a meddling, anti-liberal statism, business soon closed ranks against it. More investment was not forthcoming, growth declined, profits dropped, strikes multiplied. The employers' federation turned extremely hostile.

Meanwhile, by refusing to engage in the traditional *do ut des* of Brazil's pork-barrel politics and purging the government of its most blatantly compromised ministers, Dilma was antagonizing forces in Congress on which her majority in the legislature depended, for whom corruption was a condition of existence. After close-grained analysis of the fractions of capital, Singer situates these tensions in a striking overview of the *longue durée* of the party structure in Brazil, from the post-war period to the present. Throughout, three components persisted. From 1945 to 1964, when the military seized power, there was a party on the liberal right of the spectrum, representing bankers, urban middle classes and a section of the rural oligarchy, the UDN; a popular party on the left of the spectrum, the PTB, appealing to the working-class and urban poor; and an intermediate party, the PSD, based on the larger part of the traditional landowning class and its dependents in the countryside and smaller provincial towns. Singer dubs this last 'the party of the interior', an amoeba-like force with no distinct ideological identity, neither right nor left nor centre, slithering in whichever direction

temporary power and emoluments, democratic or undemo-
cratic, lay. Twenty years later, after the military stepped down,
this trio essentially reappeared in the shape of the PSDB, PT
and PMDB. Neither of the first two could govern without the
parasitic assistance of the third, with its wide-flung capillary
network of local office-holders, and nearly continuous control of
the powerful presidency of the Senate. Any hint of republicanism
was anathema to it.

What of the PT's own constituency? Although, ever since
1945, a pole of capital and a pole of labour were clearly discern-
ible within the political system, conflict between them was always
overdetermined by a vast sub-proletariat, urban and rural, living
in pre-modern conditions whose existence skewed the system
away from a class confrontation to a populist opposition between
the rich and poor, in which the poor were as available for demagogic or clientelist capture by politicians of conservative as they
were of radical stamp. By 2006 Lula's social policies, dramatically
reducing poverty, had for the first time made this mass, much
of it subsisting in the informal economy, an electoral bastion of
the PT, which Dilma inherited. Millions had been lifted from
acute hardship and knew to whom they owed it. But, egged
on by interested journalists and the ideology of the time, the
regime took to boasting of its achievement as the creation of a
'new middle class' in Brazil, when in fact the social promotion
of most of those affected was not only more modest—formal
jobs and higher minimum wages raising them to something like
the position of a new working class—but also more precarious.
Politically, Singer argues, the official propaganda boomeranged:
its effect was to invite identification with the consumerist indi-
vidualism of the actual middle class, rather than with the existing
working class.

Once growth went negative, downward mobility struck many of those just risen. Frustration at this reversal of expectations was particularly sharp among youth who had gained from the popular expansion of higher education, however indifferent in quality, that had been another of the benefits extended by the PT to the poor, and who now found they had no access to the kind of jobs for which they had been led to hope. Here was the combustible mass that became critical in the great street uprising of June 2013—some 1.5 million in the protests at their height—that would be the watershed in the fortunes of Dilma and her party. Singer's meticulous breakdown of its participants—statistics beyond the dreams of Marx's time—shows that 80 per cent of those who marched in the demonstrations were youths or young adults, below the age of forty. Eighty per cent had been or were involved in some form of higher education, as against 13 per cent of the population as a whole; yet half had incomes of no more than between two and five minimum wages, where under two wages is the poverty line. Those below it, the sub-proletariat proper—comprising half the population—were marginal in the events, making up less than a sixth of the explosion. Decisive in the evolution and outcome of the protests, however, was the ability of the other third of the marchers, the true middle class, to secure the support of the half that believed itself or aspired to be middle class too, in a generalized indignation against the government, and beyond it the political class as a whole—dynamic activists of a youthful new right mobilizing social media to bond the two together as a force. Structurally, though not sociologically, it might be said that in Singer's vivid account the uprising of 2013 occupies a position not unlike *la pègre* in Marx's account of 1848.

The victors who captured the movement, and made it into a springboard for what would become much larger and more deadly assaults on the government two years later, were the newest cohorts of the urban middle class in the big cities in the south of the country. Big business, the working class and the poor had all benefited from PT rule. Professionals, middle management, service personnel and small employers had not. Their incomes had increased proportionately less than that of the poor, and their status had been eroded by new forms of popular consumption and social mobility, undermining deference. Taking for granted a traditional hierarchy, with its colour connotations, and the availability of the largest number of domestic servants per capita in the world (over seven million of them) this stratum had always been a breeding-ground of reaction. Formally comprising the 'modern' sector of Brazilian society, it was of sufficient size to have long exercised a veto on changes that would make the rest of the country less backward. But if it was large enough to frustrate social inclusion of the poor in national development, it was too small to have much hope of dominating presidential elections, once the suffrage was extended after the war. It was therefore always tempted to short-circuit these in a coup. In 1964 much of the urban middle class had conspired with officers to launch a military coup. In 2016 it mounted a parliamentary coup, overthrowing the president within the framework of the constitution, rather than suspending it.

This time it was not the military, but the judiciary that acted as the lever for an overturn which this stratum, organized simply in electoral terms, as a party or set of parties, could not achieve. Magistrates, closer in their career and culture to the civilian mass of the middle class than officers, were more organic allies in a common cause. Dissenting from both of the opposite characterizations current in Brazil of the role of the judges in Lava Jato—either fearless scourges of corruption, impartially upholding the rule of law, or ruthless manipulators of it for partisan political ends—Singer views their operations as at once genuinely republican in effect, yet unmistakeably factious in direction. Republican: how else could the imprisonment of the richest and most powerful tycoons in the land be described? Not without reason, another of the operations of Lava Jato was named, after the indignant response of a Petrobras boss on being put under arrest, *Que pais é esse?*—'What kind of country is this?' Factious: how else could the systematic targeting of the PT, and sparing of other parties till Dilma was brought down, be described? Not to speak of the blurting of political sympathies and antipathies on Facebook, the smirking photo-ops of Moro with ornaments of the PSDB and the rest. The contradiction was a inextricable knot, entangled with that of the PT itself: the judges 'factious *and* republican', the party 'created to change institutions *and* swallowed by them'.[3]

Having laid out the course on which Dilma embarked on taking office, the economic and legislative obstacles into which it ran, the party system in which it was encased, the array of class forces confronting it, and the judicial siege that eventually encircled it, Singer ends with a graphic narrative of the sequence of moves and counter-moves by the individual political actors in the hurly-burly towards impeachment that finished her off. Here personalities are given full weight. Dilma's intentions were more than honourable. She wanted to advance, not just preserve, the social gains achieved by the PT under Lula, and to free them from the connivances with which they had been bought. But politically ill at ease, she compensated with rigidity, and though in private she could be relaxed and charming enough, in office

---

3   *O Lulismo em crise. Um quebra-cabeça do período Dilma (2011–2016)*, São Paulo 2018, p. 261.

she brooked neither criticism nor advice. For Singer, she must be held responsible for two fatal and avoidable errors, in each case refusing to heed her mentor. The first was her decision to stand for president a second time in 2014, rather than stepping down to allow Lula to return, as he had expected and wished to do. Out of a culpable vanity, or a natural pride in the autonomy of her project? At one point, Lula publicly allowed that he would be a candidate if there was a danger of the PSDB making a comeback, as there soon was. But personal bluntness was not his style: he never raised the matter directly with her. The political convention in Brazil, as in the US, is that an incumbent president runs for a second term, and he respected it.

The second charge against Dilma was her rejection of any deal with Cunha to save herself from impeachment, which Lula believed a necessity and sought to reach. For Singer, there lay the critical difference of character. Politically, he observes, Lula would bend, but not break; Dilma would break rather than bend. Blackmailers are never satisfied, she said: yield, and they will always come back for more. Without putting it in so many words, Singer sides with Lula. Politics as a vocation, wrote Weber, requires acceptance of 'ethical paradoxes'. Citing him, Singer suggests that this was an obligation—his word—that Dilma declined. It was such because the consequences of not bending were so grave. In stubbornly resisting a deal, she opened the door to a 'retrogression of the nation of unpredictable proportions'.[4]

In an otherwise magisterial reconstruction of Dilma's downfall, these concluding judgments seem questionable. Singer, it might be said, is both a touch too uncritical, and too critical, of Dilma. What tells against the attribution of a clear-cut republicanism to her, at any rate at the start, are the two key advisers

---

4   *O Lulismo em crise*, p. 295.

she chose when she ran for president the first time, and installed next to her when she won. Head of her campaign, and then chief of staff in Brasília, was the most notoriously corrupt single politician in the ranks of the PT, Antonio Palocci, toast of big business when he was Lula's minister of finance, before being forced to resign after a particularly ugly scandal in 2006.[5] His reappearance in 2010 was greeted with delight by the *Economist*, but it soon emerged that in the interim he had acquired a massive unexplained fortune in consultancies and real estate operations, and Dilma had to get rid of him. Predictably, this abject figure would then be the only PT leader to turn delator in Lava Jato. After he was gone, João Santana remained by her side: her most intimate counselor, and by many accounts a critical influence on her decisions. Once a songwriter in a back-up group for Caetano Veloso, then a star investigative reporter, before becoming the top-paid *marqueteiro*—all-purpose commercial campaign manager and brand-fabricator—in the country, Santana was put into marketing orbit by Palocci in his home town and plied his services on an international scale; among his clients was the billionaire presidential looter of Angola, José Eduardo dos Santos. He lasted six years with Dilma, before Lava Jato caught up with him for a $10 million bribe he had salted away in Panama. Naturally, being a mercenary, he too bought leniency with delation. In both cases, Dilma's judgment was less than republican. Not herself a product of the PT, which she had joined only in 2001, she could not so easily escape its habitus.

On the other hand, the criticisms that she damaged the party by not passing the baton to Lula in 2014, and endangered

---

5   Lula has specifically denied he was responsible for the selection of Palocci as chief of staff in 2014: it was Dilma's choice, which he opposed: *A verdade vencerá*, São Paulo 2018, p. 35.

the country by refusing the pact with Cunha he urged in 2016, imply two counterfactuals against which the logic of the historical situation speaks. Had Lula rather than Dilma run against Aécio in 2014, he would certainly have won by a wider margin, and would have been unlikely to make such a clumsily abrupt turn towards austerity, alienating the poor, as she did. But the economic conjuncture did not permit a repetition of the stimulus that allowed him to ride out the global financial crisis of 2008 as a mere 'ripple' in Brazil. The commodities super-cycle was over, all economic signals were pointing down: the poison pills left by his own rule were being consumed. Furthermore, the storm of Lava Jato would have hit his presidency with yet greater force than it did Dilma's. Personally, he was much more exposed to its attack. There would have been no need to resort to budgetary technicalities for an impeachment: inevitably it would have been much more broadside, with even more deafening clamour on the streets and screens of the country. His traditional political skills in handling Congress might still have averted a fate that he had escaped once before, at the time of the *mensalão*, in the best of cases perhaps allowing him to limp to the end of his term. But the price would have been three years of being manacled with Cunha in such common moral-political odium that, in all likelihood, retribution at the polls in 2018 would have been even more devastating. There were good reasons why not just Dilma, but the PT itself, rejected collusion with Cunha. The price in credibility, which was already so damaged, was too high, the pay-off too fleeting.

The judges themselves, of course, had scarcely more scruple in tolerating Cunha, so long as he held the keys to impeachment, than the politician they had in their sights. Singer's account of the outlook and impact of the magistrates of Lava Jato is a model of level-headed analysis. Still, it leaves two questions open. Republican yet factious, yes: but what would be the ultimate balance between the two—merely of equal effect? Were these, moreover, the only two elements in the make-up of the Brazilian judiciary? Singer's focus is on the pool in Curitiba. But it was operating within a legal system that predated and overtopped it. There, of decisive importance was the relationship between police, prosecutors and judges. Formally speaking, each is a body independent of the other. Police gather evidence, prosecutors bring charges, judges pronounce verdicts (in Brazil juries exist only for cases of homicide). In practice, however, Lava Jato fused these three functions into one, prosecutors and police working under the supervision of the judge, who controlled investigations, determined indictments and delivered sentences. The negation of ordinary principles of justice in such a system, even without Moro's dismissal of presumption of innocence, is plain: powers of accusation and condemnation are no longer distinguished.

To these, moreover, were added in the course of these years three further powers. *Delacão premiada*—informing for a reward—introduced the practice, extended from judges to prosecutors, of threatening persons under arrest with crushing sentences unless they implicated others in whom the investigation was interested: in effect, judicial blackmail. The scale of abuse to which this power gives rise can be read off from the treatment accorded the wealthiest magnate netted by Lava Jato. Marcelo Odebrecht was sentenced to nineteen years in prison for corruption to the tune of $35 million. Once he turned informer, these were reduced to two and a half, and he was released from jail without further ado. The incentive to supply whatever claims might be useful for other cases the magistrate is seeking to prosecute is obvious. Judges can even bestow pardons for them.

A further facility afforded them was abolition of the rule that appeal procedures had to be exhausted before an accused could be imprisoned.

Last but not least was the adoption, dating essentially from the *mensalão* trial, of the concept of *domínio de fato*—condemnation in the absence of any direct evidence of participation in a crime, on the grounds that the accused must have been in charge of it. This was the basis on which Lula's chief of staff Dirceu was sentenced, for his hierarchical position as the head of political administration in Brasília. The notion was borrowed from the principle of *Tatherrschaft*, developed by the German jurist Claus Roxin for Nazi war crimes. Roxin, however, has protested against Brazilian abuse of it: organizational position did not suffice for the crime as he defined it, there had to be some proof of giving a command.[6] Moro, however, dispensed even with organizational hierarchy, in deploying *domínio de fato* to convict Lula of the intention of receiving an apartment from Odebrecht which he never used or owned. The value of the property was $600,000 dollars, for which he was jailed for twelve years: over two-thirds of Odebrecht's punishment, for less than 2 per cent of the sum for which Odebrecht was charged. The ratios speak for themselves.

In such cases, as processed in Curitiba, the combination of republican zeal and factious bias applies. Moving up the judicial ladder to Brasília, where the Supreme Court (STF) presides at the top of it, the same cannot be said. There, neither ethical rigour nor ideological fervour are anywhere in sight: motivations are of an altogether different, more squalid order. Unlike its counterparts anywhere else in the world, the STF combines

---

6 Livia Scocuglia, 'Claus Roxin critica aplicação atual da teoría do domínio do fato', *Boletim de Notícias ConJur* [Consultor Jurídico], 1 September 2014.

three functions: it interprets the constitution, acts as the last court of appeal in civil and criminal cases and, crucially, is alone empowered to try public officials—members of Congress and ministers—who otherwise enjoy immunity from prosecution, popularly known as *foro privilegiado,* in all other courts of the land. Its eleven members are appointed by the executive; their confirmation by the legislature, quite unlike in the US, is no more than pro forma. Previous experience on the bench is not required—only three of the current justices have any; mere practice as a lawyer or a prosecutor, with a smattering of academic credentials, is the usual background.

Though chosen by the government of the day, serving till mandatory retirement, selection has traditionally been based not so much on ideological affinity as personal connexion: of the current batch, one is a former lawyer for Lula, another a crony of Cardoso, a third a cousin of his disgraced predecessor Collor. The case load of the court is grotesque, with over 100,000 cases before it in 2017, allocated for preliminary consideration by lottery to individual judges, each vested—no other Supreme Court in the world features this—with arbitrary power to stall or to speed a case as they please, delaying some for years, expediting others post-haste. In practice, there are no deadlines. When a case is cleared for decision by the plenum, hearings are not only public, but—another unique feature—televised live, if the incumbent president of the court, who rotates, sees fit. In such sessions, decorum is at a minimum, grand-standing at a premium.

By the time pressure for impeachment began to build up, eight of the eleven members of the court had been picked by Lula or Dilma. But since appointments had seldom been highly political in a partisan sense, only one member of the court had a clear-cut ideological profile, as a hawk for the PSDB: Cardoso's intimate Gilmar Mendes. The rest were not of any particular colour, egoism and opportunism generally counting for more than any other –ism. But once the third function of the court, trial of politicians, acquired a salience it had never known before, from the *mensalão* onwards, those who owed their appointment to Lula and Dilma were on their mettle to show their independence of the PT. It was the first black member of the court, Joaquim Barbosa, put there by Lula, who handed down sentences of unprecedented harshness on PT cadres in the *mensalão* trial. But as events were to show, this was not so much independence in the sense of an impartial justice, as substitution of a rather nominal dependence on patrons by a more telling submission to the media.

From the start, the pool in Curitiba used leaks and planted stories in the press to short-circuit due process, convicting targets before trial in public opinion, in accord with the Brazilian wisdom—valid, of course, across the world—that 'public opinion is what gets published'. Such leaks are juridically forbidden. Moro employed them scot-free, systematically. He could do so, because the media which he used as his megaphone intimidated the judges of the STF, who feared denunciation of themselves if they demurred. When Moro was instructed by one justice on the court that on habeas corpus grounds he must release a Petrobras director he was holding in prison, he simply went to the media, explaining that if so he must release drug traffickers too. His superior immediately backed down. When he broke no less than three regulations in tapping and publishing the phone-call between Lula and Dilma, and received a feeble reprimand from the same judge, he retorted that he had acted in the public interest, and—since he was now fêted in the press as a national hero—suffered not even a slap on the wrist.

Craven in covering illegalities below, the STF was no better—servility and self-interest competing—in performance of its tasks above. If the attorney-general brings charges against a member of Congress or the government, the Court determines whether to hold a trial, its decision requiring ratification by Congress to be acted on. Charges were brought against Cunha as soon as his Swiss accounts were revealed. The Court did not stir for six months, until he had set impeachment in motion. Then it not only accepted the indictment overnight, but eager to obfuscate its inaction, peremptorily ordered his dismissal as Speaker, which it had no constitutional authority to do. As Cunha remarked with cynical accuracy: 'If it was urgent, why it did take them six months?'[7] When a PT—former PSDB—Senator was caught on tape discussing ways of spiriting a Petrobras boss out of prison, the Court acted with lightning speed, arresting him within twenty-four hours. Why? To cover its own embarrassment: he had let drop he was on terms with the judges, and sounding them out on the case. His fate? Once he offered due delation, charges were quietly dropped, and he was restored to the Senate. In its lack of any principled compass, a critic has observed, a Supreme Court which was supposed to be a power moderating tensions in the Constitution, had become—a stronger word is in order than his—an abscess generating them.[8]

Holding out for less than eighteen months before she was evicted from the Presidential Palace, Dilma's second mandate was barren of achievement. Temer's annexation of it, lasting twice as long, was altogether more consequential. Acting with

---

7   'Por unanimidade, STF afasta Eduardo Cunha da Câmara', *noticias uol. com*, 5 May 2016.

8   Conrado Hübner Mendes, 'Na prática, ministros do STF agridem a democracia', *Ilustríssima*, 28 January 2018: much the best portrait of the current Court.

a speed and resolve that made clear the depth of the planning behind impeachment, the new regime passed three classical pieces of neo-liberal statecraft in short order, altering the economic constitution of the country at a stroke. Within a month of Dilma's suspension, legislation freezing social expenditures for twenty years—no increase beyond the rate of inflation—was in front of Congress. No sooner was it passed with a two-thirds majority than the country's labour code was comprehensively scrapped: the legal limit of a working day was extended from ten to twelve hours, permissible lunch break cut from an hour to thirty minutes, protection of employees, full or part-time, reduced; check-off of union dues abolished; plus sundry other deregulations of the labour market. The new rules gave a generalized green light to outsourcing of employment and zero-hour contracts. Next up was radical pension reform, increasing contributions and raising retirement ages, to bring down the costs of constitutionally mandated social security in the name of reducing the national debt. Since beneficiaries of the most lavish payments under the existing system come from the top ranks of the bureaucracy and political class, this was a trickier proposition.

But before it could come to a vote, Temer looked within an ace of following Dilma out of office. In the spring of 2017 he was taped in a secret meeting with Joesley Batista, head of the giant corporation JBS, in the garage of the Presidential Palace discussing hush money to Cunha—who had just been sentenced and could implicate him in any number of corrupt schemes— unaware that his interlocutor was collaborating with the police. The tape was immediately broadcast on national television by Globo, to an uproar without precedent. In the same week, one of his aides could be seen on screen receiving a suitcase containing 500,000 *reais* from an emissary of Batista. For the Supreme

Court to act on the charges immediately laid against him by the attorney-general, the House had to authorize proceedings by a two-thirds vote. Beyond shame, a majority rejected any investigation.

Two months later, the attorney-general sent the STF a much wider indictment of Temer along with six other PMDB leaders, three of them already behind bars—one caught with a cash hoard of R$51 million in banknotes in his home. Once again, the House blocked any action. A year later, yet another major scandal exploded, federal police bringing charges of long-standing corruption in the docks at Santos against Temer. By then, paralyzed politically by over a year of protecting himself, though he had survived every revelation he had no agenda left. The conventional stabilization plan accompanying his initial neo-liberal measures had ended the Dilma recession, but the pick-up was weak—growth asthmatic, living standards depressed, 13 million unemployed. Temer's own credibility sub-zero, his party ran the finance minister who had presided over this recovery as its candidate for the presidency in 2018. He got 1 per cent of the vote. Yet this muted interim had, all the same, cleared the way for a high-pitched obbligato to come.

II

By mid 2016, the rule of the Workers' Party had sunk under the dual mill-stones of economic deterioration and political corruption. But by the end of 2017, the (no longer P) MDB had fallen even lower in the polls, for the same two reasons. Since the PSDB was part of Temer's support system along with the PMDB, with prominent members of the party in the government, it too could not escape the stench—Aécio, its chairman, had been taped demanding a large bribe from Joesley's corporation, and like Temer had only avoided trial by the STF through the protection of a Congress packed with confederates. In this devastated landscape, Lula—for all the sentence pronounced on him, still on appeal—remained far the most popular politician in the country, and if nothing were done about it, the most likely victor in the oncoming presidential election. With unprecedented speed—the average time for judging an appeal was cut by three-quarters to eliminate the danger—the verdict not just confirming but increasing his sentence was handed down in January 2018. For two months his lawyers were able to delay his imprisonment, and in the respite he gave a set of three extended interviews published as a book, *A verdade vencerá* [The Truth Will Triumph] in March. The title is misleading, suggesting a rebuttal of charges against him which are scarcely mentioned in what becomes a memorable, often moving, self-portrait of a politician of exceptional intuition and realist intelligence, that explains why his return to power was so resisted by the Brazilian elites.

As a ruler, Lula's operating style and political creed were one. He was a trade-unionist who had learnt back in the early eighties not 'to make demands of the type "80 per cent or nothing". That way you end up with nothing'. On becoming president in a huge, complex society in 2002, he was always aware that 'I could never treat the country wishing it were as I am'. It followed that 'to govern is to negotiate'.[9] In opposition, you could be principled. But once you win elections, if you don't have a majority in parliament, which no president had enjoyed for many years, 'you have to put your principles on the table to make them practicable'. That meant dealing with adversaries as well as allies,

---

9   Luiz Inácio Lula da Silva *A verdade vencerá. O povo sabe por que me condenam*, São Paulo 2018, p 85.

who wanted quid pro quos—offices, above all. Every predecessor had had to do the same. The PMBD was not even the worst such partner; twenty smaller intermediate parties could add up to a majority in Congress, needing to be cozened. 'You make an agreement with who is there, in Congress. If they are robbers, but have votes, you either have the courage to ask for them, or you lose'.[10] Dilma should have made a deal with Cunha. There was no feasible alternative.

But negotiation was one thing, conciliation was another. Asked whether he had not been too conciliatory as president, Lula's reply was emphatic. 'A government of conciliation is one where you can do more and don't want to do it. When you can only do less and end up doing more, it's almost the beginning of a revolution—and that's what we did in this country'.[11] He had made only such concessions as the situation required. The PT had less than one-fifth of Congress. Had he ever controlled the governorships of twenty-three states and a majority in the Constituent Assembly, like the PMDB in 1988, he would have conceded less and accomplished much more. Even so, 'we gave the people a standard of living that many armed revolutions never achieved—and in a mere eight years'. He had ended with opinion polls in the skies. But his pride was not to have been a popular president. 'What I am proudest of is to have changed the relation of the State with society, and of government with society. What I wanted to achieve as president was that the poorest in the country could imagine themselves in my place. That I did'.[12]

It is an impressive claim. Lula's largeness—and quickness—of

---

10 Ibid., pp. 136–7.
11 Ibid., p. 28.
12 Ibid., pp. 144, 141.

mind and feeling come across vividly throughout the exchanges. Self-critical they are not. Did he pick the wrong successor? He chose Dilma because she was a tough, efficient chief of staff who gave him some peace and quiet in the Presidential Palace. He knew she was politically inexperienced, but aware that she was better educated than he was, he believed she would learn; only later did he realize that she didn't actually enjoy politics, but he wasn't wrong to have selected her. Unacknowledged is his probable assumption that just because she was a novice, she would be easier to control than any seasoned cadre of the PT. Nor, more significantly, is there any sense that the dark arts of acquiring mercenary support in Congress imposed not just limits on what he could do—which he admits—but costs to his own party, as it became itself infected by them, which he doesn't. Projected onto the plane of national politics, the model of economic negotiation he brought from his trade-union background lost its innocence, and bred illusion. Wage agreements don't involve back-handers to employers. Still less, where power is at stake, can adversaries be trusted not to go *va banque*.

In a final poignant exchange, after Lula declares that if he returns to power, he will do more—go further—than he did earlier, and his opponents know it, he is asked whether he reckons a return is even possible at this point—he was within a month of serving nine years. This is his wistful reply: 'Oh, I want to come back. That depends on whether God gives me health, keeps me alive; and it depends on the understanding of members of the Judicial Power who are going to vote, whether they take care to read the records of the case and see the dirty tricks being played there.'[13] To the last, Lula believed a deal could be reached that would allow him to run again: that was how

---

13 Ibid., p. 143.

negotiations ended. He had fatally underestimated his enemies. They were determined to eliminate him. In April 2018 an ultimate plea for habeas corpus, which would have enabled him to run for the presidency, went to the Supreme Court. The Brazilian Constitution states that no criminal conviction can be executed until it is definitive—that is, all instances of appeal have been exhausted, of which in Lula's case there were two further levels. The head of the army warned that granting him habeas corpus would threaten the stability of the country, which it was the duty of the Armed Forces to defend. Whereupon the judges did their own duty with alacrity, overturning the constitutional principle by a vote of by 6:5 to bar Lula's candidacy.[14]

In the arena thus cleared, the presumptive front-runner for the presidency became the PSDB candidate Geraldo Alckmin, long-time Governor of São Paulo. A wooden figure devoid of charisma, he had lost against Lula in 2006, but was less compromised by support for Temer than his rivals in the party, and enjoyed solid backing from business. The PT was paralyzed, incapable of entering the ring since it still insisted, despite its patent impossibility, that Lula remained its candidate. At the starting gate in the opinion polls, an outsider led the field with a modest 15 per cent support: Jair Bolsonaro, a lone-wolf deputy so isolated he had received just four votes out of 513 when he ran for Speaker in 2017. Marginality in Congress was not, however, necessarily a disadvantage in running for president. Never having belonged to any of the major parties in Congress—roaming between seven smaller ones—nor held any government office, he was untainted by blame for economic hardship or ongoing

---

14 The decisive sixth vote came from Rosa Weber, a judge nominated by Dilma, who explained that her 'individual conviction' must give way to 'institutional reason': the army had spoken.

exposure for corruption, and free to attribute the ills of the former to the latter, castigating the whole political class for both. But his praise of the dictatorship and its torturers, and vituperations at large, appeared such conspicuous handicaps that it was generally assumed that once campaigning got under way, he would be relegated to the also-rans.

Alckmin, by contrast, had not just the PSDB behind him, but promptly the entire so-called *Centrão*, the swamp of intermediate-sized parties of which Lula complained, giving him half of all TV time assigned to party commercials—in the past a priceless asset. With this, he was widely expected to overwhelm Bolsonaro and other potential rivals. Seven television debates, featuring all the candidates with a minimum representation in Congress, were scheduled once campaigning started. Starting in August, they exposed Bolsonaro's disadvantage in the medium: poorly prepared and ill at ease, he was ineffectual. The more he was exposed to it, the flakier he was likely to look. In the first week of September, however, this danger was suddenly lifted. Stabbed by a mental case at a provincial rally and rushed to hospital for an emergency operation, he spent the rest of the campaign safely in bed-ridden recovery, shielded not only from debates and interviews, but the demolition that Alckmin's managers had been readying on their TV slots—official sympathy for a victim who had nearly lost his life now precluded anything so tasteless.

The PT, meanwhile, had been wasting months in futile protestations that Lula remained its candidate, and so lacked even a symbolic presence in the first debates. It was not until five days after Bolsonaro was removed from these that it came to terms with reality and produced a candidate able to run. Its choice was dictated by Lula. Fernando Haddad had for six years been minister of education, where he was widely regarded as a success, responsible for one of the major achievements of PT rule, expansion of the university system and of access to it for the poor. Young and personable, he could have made a much better, more logical successor than Dilma. But he had three handicaps: he was from São Paulo, where older and more powerful heavy-weights of the PT, jealous of their precedence, held sway; he came from an area of the party to the left of Lula's centre of it; and by background he was an academic—trained in philosophy and economics, teaching political science—set among trade-unionists who distrusted professors.

In 2012 he was instead elected mayor of São Paulo. There he soon fell foul of Dilma, who refused to listen to his plea to raise petrol prices rather than inflict higher bus fares on the city, setting off the protests of 2013 that began her undoing and ended his prospects of re-election (in Paris on a mayoral junket when they started, his own first reactions to them were coercive and dismissive).[15] He continued to lack any significant base of his own within the PT, whose functionaries had reason to distrust him. As early as 2003, in a prophetic article written as the PT took power, he had warned of the danger that rather than uprooting the old, deeply engrained patrimonialism of the Brazilian state, it could be captured by it—not, contrary to the views of Cardoso and others, by modern capitalism exploiting the archaisms of a former slave society, but the other way around: an archaic oligarchic system appropriating a modern capitalism for what was of instrumental use to it, preserving the traditional pattern of its power by saturating public authority with its private

15 See his detailed, revealing account of relations with Dilma when he was mayor: Fernando Haddad, 'Vivi na pele o que aprendi nos livros', *Piauí* 129, June 2017, pp. 28–37.

interests.[16] By 2018, amidst the patrimonial shipwreck that had overtaken the PT, his foresight and honesty stood out, and Lula, knowing he was clean and imaginative, imposed him on the party.

The ensuing campaign was a strangely asymmetric one. Starting late, Haddad was cramped by the circumstances of his appointment. With less than a month to go before the first round of the election, he had to establish a national profile of his own, against charges that he was a mere dummy for Lula, while at the same time drawing as effectively as possible on Lula's continuing popularity and prestige. It rapidly became clear that it was he and Bolsonaro who would face off in the second round, but there was no confrontation between the two. Haddad toured the country, addressing crowds, while Bolsonaro lay at home tweeting. With a fortnight to go to the first round, they were level-pegging in predictions for the second. Then, in the last few days, Bolsonaro suddenly shot ahead, to a closing lead of 46 to 29 per cent. With a gap as large as this, the second round was a foregone conclusion. The Brazilian establishment closed ranks behind the future victor. Haddad fought valiantly on, eventually halving the gap. But the final result left no doubt of the scale of Bolsonaro's triumph. Winning 55 to 45 per cent, he took every state and every major city in the country outside the north-eastern redoubt of the PT; every social class with the exception of the poorest, living on incomes of less than two minimum wages a month; every age group save the cohort between eighteen and twenty-four; and close to half of all women. Across the country, the Right jubilated in the streets. Yet there had been no great rush to the polls. Voting is compulsory in Brazil, but close to a

---

16 'Um ato expropriatório', *Reportagem*, January 2003.

third of the electorate—42 million voters—opted out, the highest proportion in twenty years.[17] The number of spoilt ballots was 60 per cent higher than in 2014. A few days earlier, an opinion poll asked voters their state of mind: 72 per cent replied 'despondent', 74 per cent 'sad', 81 per cent 'insecure'.[18]

In that last response lay, in all probability, the key to Bolsonaro's sweep. The recession had certainly been critical in the melting away of support for the PT since 2014. Corruption, which had not mattered to the poor when their living standards were rising, did when they were falling and the two could be directly connected, in nightly representations on television of huge sewers swilling with torrents of bank-notes—money stolen from hospitals, schools and playgrounds, in the discourse of Lava Jato. But the substratum of popular reactions to these images was insecurity, physical and existential. Notoriously, daily violence—traditional in the feudatory North-East, modern since the arrival of the drug trade in the South-East—takes 60,000 lives a year, a homicide rate exceeding the killings in Mexico. Police killings account for 10 per cent of these deaths. Less than 10 per cent of murders are elucidated, over 90 per cent committed with impunity. Yet the prisons are teeming: 720,000 people in jail. Two-fifths of inmates, under provisional arrest, await trials that can take two, three or more years to be held. Nearly half the Brazilian population is white; 70 per cent of those murdered, and 70 per cent of those imprisoned, are not. With drugs have come gangs, among the most powerful in the world. In 2006, the Primeiro Comando da Capital (PCC) shut down large parts of the city of São Paulo in an uprising against the police, mounted

17 'Eleições 2018', *O Globo*, 30 November 2018.
18 'Entre brigas, bolhas e boatos, medo e raiva dominan eleitores', *Folha de S. Paulo*, 28 October 2018.

from the prison cells of its leaders. But with the spread of drugs, street crime that is artisanal rather than organizational has proliferated too. Few middle-class households have never had a brush with some form of it. But they are better protected: where mugging at gun- or knife-point are commonest occurrences, the poor rob the poor.

In this jungle, the police are the most ruthless of all predators: no major crime without their take. Divided into separate 'military' and 'civilian' branches, in a ratio of about three to one, these are statewide, not federal forces. Alongside them fester informal 'militias' composed of former policemen acting as security guards or battening on the drug traffic. The small corps of federal police—a tenth the size of the military police at the disposal of the governors of São Paulo and Rio de Janeiro—is reserved largely for border control and white-collar crime. Promotion depends on arrest rates, assisted by police practices that scarcely distinguish between sale and consumption of drugs, or require witness for apprehension on the spot, offering a quick route to the criminalization of poverty, as the young and black—for these purposes, *pardo* and *preto* scarcely distinguished—are picked off for dispatch to jails where there are twice as many prisoners as places. Since miscegenation was historically so widespread, making a one-drop colour line impossible, racism in Brazil differs from the US pattern, but is no less brutal. Combined with very rapid urbanization, driven as much by the push of peasants expelled from their land as by the pull of city lights, creating pockets of huge inequality with few or no structures of reception, its effect is to displace social conflict into anomic violence. For black youth, crime can become a desperate bid for recognition, a weapon a passport to dignity—guns, rented for a few hours and pointed at the head of a driver or passer-by, becoming a means, too, of forcing them to look at, rather than away, from those otherwise treated as invisible. Successive presidents, relieved of responsibility for public security, since this remains the province of governors, have had little incentive to change what amounts to a convenient brief for inaction. At most, they can declare an emergency and send in troops to occupy slums, as a temporary exercise in public relations, typically leaving hundreds of people killed, otherwise scant trace.

For the popular classes, compounding and intersecting with the ambience of everyday violence has been disintegration of traditional norms of customary, family and sexual life, fanned not just by the diffusion of drugs, but by the media—television, vying with North American models, throwing earlier moral restraints to the winds. Women are the principal victims. Rape is as common as murder in Brazil: over 60,000 a year, 164 a day.[19] Amidst all this, economic anxieties are naturally the most permanent and intense of all—insecurity at its most fundamental level, of food and shelter. In such conditions, a desperate desire for order has increasingly been met by Pentecostal religion whose churches offer an ontological framework for making sense of lives on the edge of existence. Their trademark is a theology, not of liberation, but of 'prosperity', as the means of earthly salvation. By hard work, self-discipline, correct behavior, and communal support, believers can better themselves—and pay tithes to the pastoral organization helping them. These neo-Protestant churches typically combine shady financial corporations, making millionaires of their chief ministers, with

---

19 The number of cases reported has doubled in the past five years, but the only real sociological study, conducted in the capital cities of the North-East, makes clear how high the level of under-reporting must continue to be: see *Atlas da Violência* 2018, IPEA and FBSP, Rio de Janeiro June 2018, pp. 56–8 et seq.

the one organizational form that has effective implantation in poor neighbourhoods reached by no secular party. Today the Evangelical flocks number perhaps some 50 million Brazilians. The Pentecostal enterprises are a power in the land; in 2014 a fifth of the deputies in Congress thought it advantageous to declare an affiliation with them. Four years later, however, the conditions of their following had altered. The success of the theology of prosperity had coincided with the boom years of Lula's presidency, giving credibility to its optimism of material uplift. By 2018, the promise of steady improvement was gone. For many, everything now seemed to be falling apart.

Nowhere were these stresses more acute and concentrated than in Brazil's second city. Rio, with half the population of São Paulo, has twice the murder rate. In large part, the lesser violence in São Paulo is due to the unrivalled degree of control exercised across a city built on a plateau by the dominant *paulista* gang, the PCC, which is in a position to discourage petty assaults—complicating the orderly management of high-value drug traffic—with the heavy weapons at its disposal.[20] Rio's topography—a narrow, winding strip of coastland segmented by forest-clad mountains jutting through to the beaches, favelas crammed in their interstices, often cheek by jowl with wealthy neighbourhoods—hinders such centralized power. There rival gangs—Comando Vermelho, TCP (Terceiro Comando Puro) and others—wage fierce territorial warfare heedless of bystander casualties, and amid greater levels of poverty, a denser arms trade multiplies the random mayhem of individual hold-ups. In early

---

20 Though its stronghold is in São Paulo and the South-East, the PCC has extensive presence in the North-East and a couple of border states in the Amazon; for its growth and topography, see Bruno Paes Manso and Camila Nunes Dias, *A Guerra: a ascenção do PCC e o mundo do crime no Brasil*, São Paulo 2018, *passim*.

2018 Temer sent in the army to stopper the violence, where it has remained, as in the past to no lasting effect. In this environment, the PT was never able to take root, still less the PSDB, nor any stable partisan configuration. All three of the last governors of the state are in jail or custody for corruption. What did take political hold, with a grip more extensive than in any other big city, are the Evangelical churches. Cunha, for long Rio's dominant politician, was a lay preacher linked to the Assembly of God. Its current mayor is a pastor of the rival Universal Church of the Kingdom of God and nephew of its *capo* Edir Macedo, Brazil's (much more powerful) answer to the Reverend Moon.

Bolsonaro is a product of this petri dish. He was born in 1955 in the small-town interior of São Paulo, but his career has unfolded entirely in the state of Rio, where at the age of eighteen he entered a military academy to the south of the city in the time of the dictatorship, training as a parachutist. Rising within ten years to the rank of captain, in 1986 he published an article complaining of low salaries in the army and was arrested for indiscipline. On release he plotted a series of minor bomb explosions at various barracks to press home material discontent in the ranks. Probably because he enjoyed some protection from higher officers sympathetic to his aims, if not his methods, an investigation found the evidence against him—though it included maps drawn in his own hand—inconclusive. But he was forced to retire; he was just thirty-three. Yet with scarcely a pause, five months later he got himself elected to the city council in Rio. Within another two years, he had vaulted to Congress on the votes of the Vila Militar, an area in the west of the city built for soldiers and their families containing the largest concentration of troops in Latin America, and of the zone around the military academy where he had been a cadet.

In Brasília, he was soon calling for a regime of exception and the temporary closure of Congress, and the following year—this was 1994—declared he would rather 'survive in a military regime than die in this democracy'. Over the next two decades, his parliamentary career consisted largely of speeches extolling the military dictatorship and the armed forces; calling for the death penalty, lower jailing ages, easier access to guns; and attacking leftists, homosexuals and other enemies of society. He was returned six times, his electoral base in the barracks and their precincts holding steady at much the same level—around 100,000 votes—until 2014, when it suddenly quadrupled. The jump, little noticed at the time, was more than simply a general effect of the economic crisis, though clearly lifted by it. *Anti-petismo* had long been a powerful strain within Brazilian political culture[21] as a middle-class counterpoint to PT ascendancy, intensified as the media—above all *Veja*, the country's leading news magazine—whipped up outrage at corruption to boost the PSDB's campaigns to capture the presidency. But no-one could compete with Bolsonaro for virulence on this front. He had, moreover, learnt something from the urban uprising of 2013 that the PSDB had not. Then, young activists of a new Right in São Paulo—far ahead of their elders, or the political class generally—had pioneered use of social media to mobilize what became vast anti-government demonstrations. They were radical neo-liberals, which Bolsonaro was not, and

---

21 For this, see the important study by David Samuels and Cesar Zucco, *Partisans, Antipartisans and Nonpartisans. Voting Behaviour in Brazil*, Cambridge 2018, who emphasize the consistent levels of *anti-petismo* in the country, predating even the PT's arrival in power, little affected by growth rates under Lula, or—in their view—class markers, and driven essentially by a conservative law-and-order dislike of any too rapid political or social change.

there was little contact between the two. But he could see what they had achieved, and set up his own personal operation in Rio in advance of any competitor. By late 2017 he was far ahead of the pack, with seven million followers on Facebook, double the number of the country's leading newspaper.[22]

The success of the image he projected in this medium was a reflection not just of the violence of his pronouncements. The impression of Bolsonaro given by press coverage abroad, of an unremitting feral fanaticism, is misleading. The public personality is more ambiguous. Crude and violent certainly, but also with a boyish, playful side, capable of a coarse, on occasion even self-deprecating, good humour far from the glowering bearing of Trump, with whom he is now often compared.[23] His background was less grindingly poor than Lula's—father an unlicensed dentist plying his trade from one small town to another—but plebeian enough by the standards of the Brazilian elite. Though now well-off—owner of five properties (how acquired remains obscure)—a common touch comes naturally. His is a charisma that travels especially well among youth, both popular and more educated.

Married three times, he has four sons by the first two wives and one daughter ('a moment of weakness', he likes to joke) by the last, a volunteer for a branch-off from the Assembly of God whose televangelist leader Silas Malafaia (the third-richest pastor in Brazil, reputedly worth $150 million) married the couple,

---

22 We owe the best profile of Bolsonaro as a pre-candidate for the presidency to Consuelo Dieguez, 'Direita, Volver', *Piauí* 120, September 2016.

23 In the telling phrase of Marcus Giraldes, 'guffawing like a mixture of underworld bouncer and buffoon'. Giraldes's analysis of Bolsonaro's popular appeal, written before his victory in the second round, remains essential: 'O resultado das eleiçõese e para que serve o fascismo', *Justificando*, 19 October 2018.

before he was investigated by the federal police and she exited
to a Baptist Attitude church near their condominium. Though a
Catholic by birth, Bolsonaro has made sure of the best Evangelical
credentials, travelling with a pastor to be baptized in Israel. The
family is his political fortress. Unlike the Trump household, the
three eldest Bolsonaro sons have all made successful electoral
careers: one is now a senator for Rio, a second the most voted
deputy in history in São Paulo, a third councillor in Rio. They
are often seen as a mixture of brains-trust and bodyguard
around him, while his wife Michelle is the gate-keeper to the
outside world.

Though long a somewhat friendless loner in Congress,
Bolsonaro understood the need for allies to reach to the presidency, and showed he had the skills to acquire them. For his
running mate, he chose a four-star general, Hamilton Mourão,
just retired after becoming too outspoken. Besides openly
attacking Dilma's government, Mourão had declared that if the
judiciary failed to restore order in Brazil, the military should
intervene to do so, and floated the idea of an 'auto-coup' by
an acting president, should that be necessary; in other asides
remarked that the country needed to improve its stock, since
Indians were lazy, blacks deceitful and Portuguese spoilt. Given
that Bolsonaro's primary political base had always been military, the choice of Mourão was logical and well received in the
army. But he also needed to reassure business, wary of him not
just as a wild card, but as a congressman with a consistently
'statist' voting record, opponent of privatizations and grudging
of foreign investment. So, with a smile of engaging candour, he
confessed himself ignorant of economics, though capable of
learning from those who knew better, and found his mentor in
an economist down the road. Paulo Guedes had been trained in

Chicago, taught in Chile under Pinochet, and returned to Rio to become a successful financier.[24] He was not highly regarded by his fellow economists, and never got much of an academic job in Brazil—but he had co-founded the country's largest private investment bank and made a fortune from it, then departing for other ventures well before it was caught up in the Lava Jato investigations. A neo-liberal *pur sang*, his chief remedies for Brazil's economic ills are privatization of all state enterprises and assets to pay off the national debt, and de-regulation of every transaction in sight. With promises like these, even if some were sceptical they could so easily be kept, capital had little to complain of. Financial markets were squared. Security and economy taken care of, that left corruption. On course for victory after winning the first round, Bolsonaro dispatched Guedes to Moro to get him on board. He needed little persuasion: a few days after the second round, Bolsonaro announced that the trophy judge had accepted his invitation to become minister of justice in the incoming government. The magistrates of Mani Pulite, intending to clean up the Italian political system, put paid to the ruling parties of the First Republic, and were appalled to find they had ushered in Berlusconi. In Brazil the star judge of Lava Jato, after accomplishing much the same, was happy to join an analogue fouler by any measure.

Installed in January, the new regime marks a more radical a break with the era of the PT than the managers of Dilma's ouster, their own parties decimated at the polls, ever imagined. Central to its composition is the return of the Armed Forces to the front of the political stage, thirty years after the end of the military dictatorship. No institutional adjustment was required.

---

24 For a trenchant portrait of Guedes, see Malu Gaspar, 'O Fiador', *Piauí* No. 144, September 2018.

In the eighties, Brazilian democracy was not wrested from the generals by popular revolt, it was passed back to parliament once they considered their mission—eradication of any threat to the social order—accomplished. There was no settlement of accounts with the conspirators and torturers of 1964–85. Not only were they ensured immunity from prosecution, absolved by law from anything they had done, but their overthrow of the Second Republic was given constitutional sanction with the legalization of their rulers as regular presidents of Brazil, and acceptance of legislation by them as normal juridical continuity with the past. In all cases, the South American tyrannies of the sixties and seventies made an amnesty for their crimes a condition for withdrawing to the barracks. Once democracy was consolidated, in every other country these amnesties were partially or completely revoked. Not in Brazil. In every other country, within one to five years a Truth Commission was set up to examine the past. In Brazil it took twenty-six years before such a commission reported, and no action was taken against the perpetrators it named.[25] Indeed, in 2010 the Supreme Court declared the amnesty law nothing less than a 'foundation of Brazilian democracy'. Eight years later, in a speech commemorating the thirtieth anniversary of the Constitution enacted when the generals had left, the president of the Supreme Court, Dias Toffoli—former legal errand boy of the PT, arguably the most despicable single figure in today's political landscape, though there is a lot of competition—formally blessed their seizure of power, telling his audience: 'Today I no longer refer to a coup or a revolution. I refer to the movement of 1964'.

---

25 For particulars, see Anthony Pereira, 'Progress or Perdition? Brazil's Truth Commission in Comparative Perspective', in Peter Kingstone and Timothy Power, *Democratic Brazil Divided*, Pittsburgh 2018, pp. 152–71.

In 2018, the Army had its electoral say early on. In April, its commander-in-chief, Villas Bôas, warned against any grant of habeas corpus to Lula, in the name, as he later explained, of the most cherished value of the armed forces, the stability of the country. Bolsonaro safely elected, he hailed the new president's victory as a welcome release of national energy, and in retirement in January thanked him for 'liberation from the ideological shackles sequestering free thought' in Brazil. To discuss 1964 today was ridiculous, and the Truth Commission a disservice to the country. Questions of public security were also matters of national security. He had taken part in one of the periodic military interventions to restore order in the slums of Rio, and seen how futile civilian incompetence had made them. In that they resembled Brazilian military intervention in Haiti, which had been much too short-lived, chaos returning as soon as its troops departed.[26] Not a lesson lost on Bolsonaro, whose key first appointment was General Augusto Heleno, commander of the Brazilian forces dispatched to Haiti—to his shame, under Lula, to please Washington—in 2004 to lock down the eviction of Aristide, installing him as head of 'Institutional Security' in the Presidential Palace. Another general, also a veteran of Haiti, Floriano Peixoto is secretary-general of the presidency, a kind of super chief of staff. A third, Santos Cruz, yet another veteran of Haiti, is in charge of relations with Congress, flanked by two more officers in the Ministries of Defence and Science and Technology, and third in charge of public relations. Heleno, the most powerful of the group, has made no secret of his convictions, expressed

---

26 See 'Bolsonaro não é volta dos militares, mas há o risco de politicização de quartéis', and 'Ao passar commando do Exército, general elogia Bolsonaro por "liberar de amarras ideológicas"', *Folha*, 11 November 2018 and 11 January 2019.

in the dictum: *direitos humanos são para humanos direitos*
'human rights are for the righteous'—and nobody else. His first
pronouncement in government was to compare guns with cars
as the right of every normal citizen to possess.

The economic wing of the government, of greater concern to
financial markets, is more friable. Guedes has assembled a team
mostly of like-minded radical neo-liberals around him, greeted
with enthusiasm by business, and can build on the deregulation
Temer had already delivered. Top of the agenda is dismantling
of the existing pension system. Indefensible on any measure of
social justice, absorbing a third of tax revenues, over a half of
its total pay-outs—which start at an average age of fifty-five for
males—are taken by the most affluent fifth of the population
(judges, officers and bureaucrats prominent in their ranks), less
than 3 per cent by those who are worst-off.[27] Naturally, however,
inequity isn't the driver of standard schemes of pension reform,
whose priority in Brazil, as elsewhere, is not to redress it, but to
slash the weight of pensions in the budget, while other cuts in
public spending wait in the pipe-line. Privatizations, the other
pièce de resistance of Guedes's programme, are advertised as the
way to pay off the public debt. A hundred state holdings of one
kind or another—the plums are in infrastructure: motorways,
ports, air-fields—are scheduled for disposal or closure, naturally
also in the name of efficiency and better service, under the direction of a military engineer, another veteran of Haiti. As under
Cardoso, no doubt many of the richest pickings will go to foreign

---

27 See Table 2 in Rozanne Siqueira and José Ricardo Nogueira, 'Taxation,
    Inequality and the Illusion of the Social Contract in Brazil', World Economic
    Association Conference 2014, and—from the same authors with Evaldo
    Souza—Graph 3 in *Efeito Redistributivo da Política Fiscal no Brasil*, Brasília
    December 2017, work that should be far better known in the country than
    it is.

investors. The elated reaction of the *Financial Times* to the economic package in prospect is understandable. Why worry about a few political gaffes? 'López Obrador Is Bigger Threat to Liberal Democracy than Bolsonaro', its Latin American editor decided.[28]

This cutting-edge austeritarian overhaul of the economy requires, of course, passage through Congress. There, much Brazilian commentary expects resistance, given the dependence of so many of its members on the provision of federal funding to their localities, which austerity would undercut. Privatization, too, is often thought to be so at variance with the statist nationalism of the Brazilian military—as a deputy, Bolsonaro himself vehemently opposed it—that it is likely be watered down in practice. On both counts, some scepticism is warranted. Under the PT presidencies, the legislature was a fundamental barrier to the will of the Executive, limiting what it could do and compromising it in what it did, with notorious results. But this was the predictable product of tensions between a radical party in control of one branch of the Constitution, and a salmagundi of conservative parties in control of another. Where no comparable tension existed between president and Congress, as under the centre-right administration of Cardoso, the executive was rarely frustrated—privatizations, for example, sailing through. Bolsonaro's brand of neo-liberalism promises to be significantly more drastic, but his popular mandate for change is much greater, and opposition to it in Congress notably weaker.

There his fly-by-night Social Liberal Party, cobbled together within a few weeks of the elections, will be the largest force in the Lower Chamber, once it is topped up, as it probably will be, with desertions from the huge marsh of venal lesser groupings.

---

28 *Financial Times*, 27 November 2018; John Paul Rathbone *dixit*.

The once mighty PSDB and PMDB have been reduced to shadows of their former selves, their former representation in Congress halved. The debacle of the PSDB and its patriarch have been especially striking. Cardoso, after failing to persuade one vacuous TV presenter to run for the presidency, seeing his party's candidate get just under 5 per cent of the national vote, and refusing to support Haddad against Bolsonaro in the second round—brushing off anguished pleas for him to do so from well-meaning friends at home and abroad with a petulant 'to hell with them all'[29]—ended up with the PSDB in São Paulo, and no doubt soon nationally, in the hands of João Doria, long host of a show modelled on Trump's *Apprentice* and franchised by it. This reptilian figure ran on a ticket brazenly twinning himself with the presidential winner as 'Bolsodoria'. Poetic justice. In Congress, the bandwagon is likely to roll just as fast, deputies clambering aboard in greed or fear to give the Executive, at least to begin with, the majorities it needs. As for military resistance to privatization or foreign take-overs, the first of Brazil's generals to run the country after they seized power in 1964, Castelo Branco, was no enemy of either. His planning minister, later Brazilian ambassador in London, was the famously outspoken champion of free markets and foreign capital Roberto Campos. Bolsonaro has just appointed his grandson head of the Central Bank. To believe that sale of public assets will become much of a wedge between Bolsonaro and his praetorians could prove wishful thinking.

---

29 'Ah, vá para o inferno. Não preciso ser coagido moralmente por ninguém': see *Estadão*, 18 October 2018. His philosophical alter ego, José Giannotti, openly welcomed Bolsonaro's victory. Asked what he thought of the result of the election, he told an interviewer, 'I am happy about it', explaining that before, under the PT, the political system had been wholly closed. 'Now it's in complete disarray. Great!': *Folha*, 16 October 2018.

The more serious risk of attrition within the new regime lies elsewhere, in the unfinished business of Lava Jato. Like the old, the new Congress is packed with recipients of bribes, distributors of back-handers, ill-gotten fortunes, life-times of assiduous corruption—in not a few cases, indeed, it has become a sanctuary for those already in the cross-hairs of the police, who got themselves elected to it simply to gain immunity from prosecution. Prominent among these is Aécio, with multiple charges piling up against him. Nor are Bolsonaro and his family in the clear, investigators having—post-election—not only discovered suspicious transactions in the accounts of his son Flávio, but still more explosively, connexions linking him to an ex-captain of the military police in Rio: a thug twice charged with militia-style killings and now on the lam, who could be implicated in the murder of black legislator and activist Marielle Franco in March of last year, which caused an international outcry. Can Moro as minister of justice now pass a sponge over delicts towards which as a magistrate he owed his fame for being merciless? Already, he has explained that the Ten Measures Against Corruption, which for years he insisted must be passed if the country was to be cleansed, needed 'rethinking': not all of them were any longer so important. Yet to unwind the dynamic of Lava Jato altogether would destroy his standing. Should Congress try to pass a general amnesty for cases of corruption, a move mooted under Temer, the stage would be set for a full-tilt conflict of powers—as it also would if, vice-versa, Moro pressed the Supreme Court to lift the immunity of too many deputies. This is the front where the potential for combustion is most real.

Capping these diverse segments of the regime is the circle composed of Bolsonaro himself, his offspring and immediate entourage. Their arrival at the apex of the state marks a significant alteration in the geography of power in Brazil. After Getulio Vargas shot himself in the Catete Palace in 1954, Rio—capital of the country for some two hundred years—lost its position as the centre of national politics. Construction of Brasília started in 1957, and was completed by 1960. Thereafter, presidents came from São Paulo (Jânio, Cardoso, Lula), Rio Grande do Sul (Jango, Dilma), Minas (Itamar) or the North-East (Sarney, Collor).[30] Demoted politically, Rio declined—some would say, rotted—economically, socially and physically. Neither the PT nor the PSDB ever secured much of a foothold in the city, for long stretches an ideological no man's land, with little purchase on national politics. This started to change with the rise of Cunha to the helm of Congress, an archetypal *carioca* figure with a pack of monetized deputies at his beck and call. The new regime has consummated the shift. After six decades in which it was marginal, power has moved back to Rio. All three of the most important positions in the administration are occupied by its products—Bolsonaro in the presidency, Guedes in the Ministry of Finance, and the rotund fixer Rodrigo Maia in Cunha's seat as Speaker of the House. In the Cabinet, which for the first time in the history of the republic contains not a single minister from the North-East or the North of the country, all coming from just six out of Brazil's twenty-six states, the largest contingent—a quarter—are natives of Rio. It is a signal shift.

How is Bolsonaro then to be classified? Often heard on the Left in Brazil, and in the liberal press in Europe, is the opinion that his rise represents a contemporary version of fascism. The

---

30 Prior to the Revolution of 1930 that brought Vargas to power, the presidency under the civilian oligarchy of the Old Republic had alternated for the most part between São Paulo and Minas in the so-called *café com leite* system, the exceptions coming from Rio and Paraíba.

same, of course, is a standard depiction of Trump in liberal and left circles in America and the North Atlantic at large, if typically assorted with escape clauses—'much like', 'reminiscent of', 'resembling'—making clear that it is little more than lazy invective.[31] The label is no more plausible in Brazil. Fascism was a reaction to the danger of social revolution, in a time of economic dislocation or depression. It commanded dedicated cadres, organized mass movements and possessed an articulated ideology. Brazil had its version in the thirties, the green-shirt Integralistas, who at their height numbered over a million members, with a voluble leader, Plínio Salgado, an extensive press, publishing programme and set of cultural organizations. They came close to seizing power in 1938, after the failure of a communist insurrection in 1935. In Brazil today, nothing remotely comparable to either a danger to the established order from the Left, or a disciplined mass force on the Right, exists. In 1964, there was still a major communist party, with influence inside the armed forces, a militant trade-union movement and growing unrest in the countryside, under a weak president calling for radical reforms. That was enough to provoke not fascism but a conventional military dictatorship. In 2018, the Communist Party of old was long gone, combative trade-unions were a back number, the poor were passive and dispersed, the PT was a mildly reforming party, for years on good terms with big business. Breathing fire, Bolsonaro could win an election. But there is scarcely any organizational infrastructure beneath him, and no need for mass repression, since there is no mass opposition to crush.

Is Bolsonaro better pigeon holed as a populist? The term

---

31 For a comprehensive demolition of the label, and the literature surrounding it, see Dylan Riley, 'What Is Trump?', *New Left Review* 114, pp. 5–31.

now suffers such inflation as the all-purpose bugbear of the *bien-pensant* media that its utility has declined. Undoubtedly, his posture as a valiant foe of the establishment, and style as a rough-hewed man of the people, belong to the repertoire of what is generally viewed as populism. Modelling himself on the president of the US, Bolsonaro outdoes Trump in wrapping himself in the national flag, and spewing a twitter-stream—70 per cent more tweets than the latter in his first week in office. But in the gallery of right-wing populists today, Bolsonaro does not fit the standard bill in at least two respects. Immigration is not a significant issue in Brazil, where just 600,000 out of a population of 204 million are foreign-born[32]—0.3 per cent, compared with some 14 per cent in the US and UK, or 16 per cent in Germany. Racism, of course, is an issue, to which Bolsonaro like Trump has made covert appeals, and whose violence in the practices of the police he will encourage. But unlike Trump, he won a large black and *pardo* (mixed) constituency in the polls, and is not likely to risk this by anything approaching an equivalent of white supremacy or backlash rhetoric in the North Atlantic. A third of his party in parliament, indeed, is not white—a higher percentage than in the much-vaunted progressive Democratic contingent in the current 116th Congress. A second significant difference lies in the character of Bolsonaro's nationalism. Brazil is not a country either afflicted or threatened by loss of sovereignty as in the EU, or by imperial decline as in the US or UK, the two drivers of right-wing populism in the North. His patriotic chest-beating is more factitious. So today he is no enemy of foreign capital. His nationalism, in expression hyperbolic enough, essentially takes the form of virulent tropes of anti-socialism, anti-feminism and

---

32   José Tadeu Arantes, 'O panorama da imigração no Brasil', *Exame*, 7 July 2015.

homophobia as so many excrescences alien to the Brazilian soul. But it has no quarrel with free markets. In local parlance, it offers the paradox of a *populismo entreguista*—one perfectly willing, in principle at least, to hand over national assets to global banks and corporations.

Comparison with Trump, Bolsonaro's closest analogue as a politician, indicates a different set of strengths and weaknesses. Personally, though he comes from a much humbler background, he is less illiterate. Education in a military academy saw to that: books are not a complete mystery to him. Aware of certain of his limitations, he lacks Trump's degree of egomania. Trump's overweening confidence in himself comes not just from a millionaire family background, but a long career of success in real estate speculation and show business. Bolsonaro, who has never run anything in his life, has known no such existential build-up. He is much less secure. Given, like Trump, to every kind of intemperate outburst—his have often been the more rabid—he will, unlike Trump, quickly back off if reactions become too negative. The first weeks of his administration have been a cacophony of conflicting statements and retractions or denials of them.

It is not just in character, but by circumstance, that he is a more brittle figure. Both he and Trump catapulted to power virtually overnight, against all expectation. Trump took the presidency with a much lower percentage of the vote—46 per cent—than the 55 per cent majority Bolsonaro won. But his supporters are ideologically fervent and solidly behind him, whereas Bolsonaro's support may be wider, but is shallower, as post-electoral polls indicating rejection of many of his proposed policies show. Trump, moreover, came to power by taking over one of the two great parties of the country, with a history going back two centuries, where Bolsonaro won it effectively on his own, without any institutional support at the polls. Once elected, on the other hand, he will not, because he cannot, rule without taking account of the institutions around him, as Trump has tried to do. This doesn't mean he will be less brutal, since in Brazil many of these are more authoritarian than in the US. The indigenous peoples of the Amazon are a sure victim: unlike blacks a *quantité négligeable* at the polls, they will be the first to suffer from his rule, as cattle ranchers sweep across their habitat. So too it is easy to imagine—especially if the economy fails to pick up, and he needs to distract attention from it—Bolsonaro cracking down viciously on student protests; rounding up activists of the MST, landless invaders of latifundia, or its urban equivalent the MTST, occupier of squats, and banning their organizations; breaking strikes, where necessary. But rainforest apart, such repression is likely to be retail, not wholesale. More, for the moment, would be surplus to requirements.

Where will that leave the PT? Far from flourishing, but so far surviving. With 10 per cent of the vote and 11 per cent of the seats in the Chamber of Deputies, it avoided the rout of the PSDB and PMDB. With Lula in jail, what is likely to become of it? Here qualified opinion divides. For Singer, the central reality of the PT years was, as the titles of his two books make plain, *lulismo*—the person overshadowing the party. For the best American scholar on contemporary Brazil, David Samuels, it is the reverse: the deeper, more durable phenomenon was *petismo*—the party rather than the person. Lula, in his view, was not a charismatic leader like Vargas, or his heirs from Rio Grande do Sul, Goulart or Brizola, politicians without real roots in a party. Nor, for that matter, unlike these figures, was he a populist. Financially orthodox, respectful of democratic institutions, he neither created a political system around himself, nor gave way to inflammatory Manichaean rhetoric of 'them' and 'us'. So *lulismo* itself never amounted to more than a 'thin psychological attachment', compared to the PT's organizational strength and solid racination in civil society. Singer was wrong both to exaggerate the importance of Lula, and to attribute a generally conservative outlook to the poor, offset by a special investment in him. In 2014, Samuels and his Brazilian colleague could write: 'Peering into our crystal ball, we see the PT as the fulcrum of Brazil's party system. Without it, governance will be difficult.'[33]

Singer's predictions have worn better. Events have shown that his sense of the mentality of the dispossessed, their fear of disorder and anxious desire for stability, was accurate. In their clairvoyance, many pages from *Os sentidos do Lulismo*, noting the precedents of Quadros and Collor, read like a scenario for Bolsonaro's triumph in popular zones of Brazil six years later. What has this meant for the relations between the PT and its leader since? On the eve of his imprisonment, an interviewer remarked to Lula: 'There are those who say that the problem in Brazil is that it never knew a war, a rupture'. His answer was: 'I agree. It's funny the way each time Brazil was on the verge of a rupture, there was an agreement. An agreement reached from above. Those who are above never want to leave.'[34] The reply is revealing: what it excludes is the possibility that those above might want a rupture—a break instigated from the Right, not the Left.[35] Yet this is effectively what hit the PT in 2016–18, and

33 David Samuels and Cesar Zucco, 'Lulismo, Petismo, and the Future of Brazilian Politics', *Journal of Politics in Latin America* 3, 2014, pp. 131–3, 153–4, where *lulismo* is contrasted with *peronismo*. For reiterated disagreement with Singer, see *Partisans, Antipartisans, Nonpartisans*, pp. 34, 167.
34 *A verdade vencerá*, p. 143.
35 Singer: 'Lulismo would not prepare its base for counter-revolution, since

with which it has yet to come to terms. In power, so long as the going was good, it benefited the poor; but it neither educated nor mobilized them. Its enemies, meanwhile, not only mobilized but educated themselves, up to the latest postmodern standards. The result was a one-sided class war, which only one camp could win. The huge demonstrations that ended by toppling Dilma were the outcome of a galvanization of the middle class such as Brazil had never witnessed in its history; enabled by a mastery of social media, transmitted from its youth to Bolsonaro, reflecting a transformation of the country little short of a social revolution. Between 2014 and 2018, despite the recession, the number of smartphones surpassed the number of its inhabitants,[36] and their use would put any other political deployment of them, in Europe or America, in the shade.

That, of course, was not the only lethal reality which the PT failed to recognize. In office, it had rejected mobilization—Lula was frank about his scepticism of it[37]—in favour of co-option; and co-option—of the Brazilian political and business class— meant corruption. That was in the logic of its strategic choice in office. 'Between consent and force stands corruption', wrote Gramsci, 'which is characteristic of situations when it is hard to exercise the hegemonic function and the use of force is too

---

this implied opening a confrontation that lay outside its recipe of concili-ation': *O Lulismo em crise*, p. 279.

36　220 million smartphones to 208 million inhabitants: José Roberto de Toledo, 'Deu no celular', *Piauí*, 18 October 2018.

37　'Mobilization doesn't solve everything. We mounted the largest mobiliza-tion in the history of the country for Direct Elections [in 1984], we went to Congress, and didn't get direct elections. And nothing happened. People watched the ships go by and waited for the Electoral College in 1985. No-one is mobilizing against the trials to which they are subjecting me': *A verdade vencerá*, p. 144.

risky'.[38] Renouncing hegemony, which required a sustained effort of popular enlightenment and collective organization, and refusing coercion, towards which it never felt any temptation, the party was left with corruption. To its leaders, anything else seemed too hard or too risky. Corruption was the price of its 'weak reformism', in Singer's phrase, and the real benefits it made possible. But once it was exposed, the party could find no words to name and criticize what it had done. Instead, in an all too revealing—in its way, disastrously accurate—euphemism, it explained that it needed to 'overcome its adaptation to the modus vivendi of traditional Brazilian politics'.[39] *Modus vivendi*—a way of living together: just so.

Resort to euphemisms offers no escape from a past to which the PT remains fettered, in the most painful and paralyzing way. For Lava Jato is far from finished with its star victim. Lula's twelve-year sentence for his inspection of a beach-side condominium is just the beginning. A second trial on a similar charge, employing a construction firm that had received government contracts while he was in office for improvement of a friend's retreat, is currently nearing conclusion, with a similar verdict in view. These charges are still, in the sum of things, relatively trivial, though the sentences are not. Coming down the pike, however, are far more serious accusations, not of private dereliction, but malversation of huge sums of public money—hundreds of millions of dollars at the disposal of Petrobras when he was president—based on the rewarded testimony of the leading Judas of the party, his one-time right-hand man, former minister of finance, Antonio Palocci, at present selling himself as a witness on yet further cases for prosecution. The government

---

38 *Quaderni del carcere*, III, Turin 1975, p. 1638.
39 See Singer, *Lulismo em crise*, p. 260.

will ensure maximum publicity for the mega-trials to come. It needs to finish off Lula.

The PT, and its sympathizers, deeply and understandably angered at the lack of commutative justice with which Lula's personal affairs have been handled, are likely to have to confront evidence, however tainted, potentially far more damaging, in what threatens to be an indefinitely extended process to discredit and confine, for life, the former president. How is the party to react? Lula, who has not been diminished in prison, remains its overwhelmingly most important political asset; yet now one in danger of becoming, for many, almost equally a liability. To do him historical justice seems beyond its powers.[40] The party depends on him for steady leadership, but risks forfeiting credibility without independence of him. Anchor or albatross? If he were fully abstracted from the scene, many think the PT would rapidly split. In such an impasse, militants may well be driven to hope that under Bolsonaro conditions in Brazil will so much worsen that few will any longer care about the venial scandals of the past, their traces obliterated in some vaster upheaval to come.

For a dozen years, Brazil was the only major country in the world to defy the epoch, to refuse the deepening of the neo-liberal regime of capital, and relax some of its rigours in

---

40 So too, it should be said, much of the Left that attacked the PT in power. Of these years, Marcus Giraldes has written well of a shared aphasia: 'Since the defeat is that of the whole left, all of whose sectors made mistakes in one way or another, if proportionate to the influence of each, the effort of self-criticism should now be common. This holds for the organizations critical of the PT governments from the left, and also for militants devoted primarily to so-called questions of identity. It is time to come to terms—publicly, severely, honestly and fairly—with all the errors that were committed, of political behavior, reading of reality, language': 'A esquerda depois das eleições: organização, estratégias, resistência', *Justificando*, 8 November 2018.

favour of the least well off. Whether the experience had to end as it did is imponderable. The masses were not called to defend what they had gained. Did the centuries of slavery that set the country apart from the rest of Latin America make popular passivity insuperable, the PT's modus vivendi the best that could be done? At times, Singer has implied something like this. At others, he is more stringent. Brazil, he recently wrote, has failed to achieve the social inclusion of all its citizens that was the task of his generation after the dictatorship. But in its absence, no other projects are viable.[41] In a slightly more optimistic vein, another acute observer, a little to his right, Celso Rocha de Barros, has remarked that Lulismo will not be finished in Brazil until something better replaces it.[42] One must hope these judgments hold good. But memories can fade, and elsewhere, social exclusion has proved only too cruelly viable. The Left has always been inclined to make predictions of its preferences. It would be an error to count on defeat self-correcting itself with time.

---

41 'In my view, Brazil has still not incorporated the whole of its population into minimum conditions of a decent life, which means incorporating them into the most advanced economy, because this is very unequal. So long as Brazil does not complete that process, there can be no other projects. This is the fundamental problem, which at a more optimistic historical moment I thought my generation was going to see resolved, and it was not': '"Democracia brasileira se esgarçou e pode se romper" afirma André Singer', *noticias.uol.com*, 4 August 2018.

42 Celso Rocha de Barros, 'O Companheiro Impeachment', *Folha*, 2 October 2017.

6

PARABOLA

July 2019

Six months is not a long time to take the measure of a new regime, but enough in the case of Bolsonaro's presidency to form a preliminary judgment. Comparisons with Trump, at the outset based on their respective performance at the polls and depth of social support, can now be extended to their conduct in office. The most striking parallel is the chaotic turnover of appointments in the administration of each, amid a rain of random dismissals and nominations, and a downpour of tweets, seeking to bypass conventional means of communication to rouse sympathizers by direct appeal in social media. But three critical differences between the two rulers have quickly become apparent. As previously noted, if both were political novices, suddenly catapulted into power, Trump could boast a previous career both as a real-estate tycoon, however shady his dealings or shaky his empire, and as a television impresario, however tawdry his show. Bolsonaro had no experience in running anything.

Erratic and unstable, unconnected to any political organization, he was not the first Brazilian politician to capture the presidency as a ramshackle outsider. Each in their fashion, Quadros and Collor were conspicuous precedents. But they had at least some administrative experience behind them, as governor and mayor of the capital in their respective states, São Paulo and Alagoas. Bolsonaro had administered nothing.

What he did possess, unlike either of them, was an unbroken stretch of twenty-six years as a deputy in Congress. These, however, he had never used to acquire a good institutional grasp of its workings as a legislature, or a tactical network of like-minded colleagues. Rather the opposite: where Quadros and Collor entered into conflict with Congress only after taking the presidency, Bolsonaro launched his campaign for the presidency with strident attacks on Congress, as part and parcel of the corrupt system of 'old politics' his mission would be to demolish. In that, his rhetoric resembled Trump's denunciations of the 'swamp' in Washington two years earlier. But the similarity of posture only underlines the contrast in context. Where Trump came to power by capturing the Republican Party—half of the country's long-established political system, which was in no danger of melt-down—Bolsonaro's rise was the product of a virtual collapse of Brazil's traditional system, with both of its main parties, PT and PSDB, in complete disorientation after the debacle of the Dilma and Temer presidencies, and a miasma of monetary scandals hanging over the entire political class. His overnight ascent was a much more aleatory outcome of a vacuum of power.

That meant he faced considerably less opposition than Trump when he banked his victory at the polls. But the advantage was illusory, dissipated within short order as it became clear that he had no idea how to control or steer a Congress that had shifted well to the right in his wake,[1] but in which his own party, just confected for his campaign, had only 10 per cent of the seats. Rejecting the pact accepted by his predecessors—distribution of lucrative ministries and sinecures in the executive in exchanges for votes in the legislature—of so-called Presidential Coalitionism, a formula for generalized corruption, and vainly attempting to mobilize street protests against it, he rapidly antagonized the morass of deputies for hire in the Centrão, without whose support he could advance no significant legislative agenda. Until the mid-terms of 2018, Republican control of both houses of Congress put Trump in a far stronger position, if not without some attrition, too.

The most salient contrast between the two rulers, however, lies elsewhere. Bolsonaro's priority, it quickly became clear, is essentially foreign to Trump. His main preoccupation has been to prosecute his version of culture wars, at the expense of any other focus of policy or attention. As a deputy in Congress, his practical activity was confined to the continuous defense of corporate interests of the military and manufacturers of small arms, a record which attracted little notice. What gave him a national profile, if at first an isolated one, were virulent rhetorical tirades against the evils of feminism, homosexuality, atheism and, of course, communism, assorted with tributes to the torturers who had made short work of these under the dictatorship. Connecting in due course ever more closely with the rising evangelical churches in the country, by the time he became a leading candidate for the presidency this was a discourse placed stridently under the sign of God and the family. So it is that once in the

---

1   For a failure to anticipate the extent of this incapacity, see the misjudgment at p. 185 above.

Planalto, more presidential energy has been invested to date in flailing efforts to stamp out aberrant ideas—sex education and the like—in schools, and to cut down study of subversive humanities in the universities, along with provision of wholesome access to firearms for the self-defence of every citizen, than to any economic, social, environmental or foreign-policy issue, in one bizarre initiative or outburst after another.[2] Right-wing enough, such hysterical moralism—however artificial—is not something Trump had any interest in, or, for obvious reasons, could afford.

From this baseline, what has been the impact of Bolsonaro's style of rule—a general political amateurism, gesticulations of prepotence and lapses into impotence, obsession with ideological phantasms—on the sociological tripod that raised him to power: business, the judiciary, the military? Capital, believing it had first claim on him, celebrated his arrival in the Planalto with a burst of (speculative rather than productive) animal spirits: in the first six months of 2019, the stock market jumped 10 per cent on the expectation of privatization and welfare cuts, hitting an all-time high in March. The key to future confidence was the promise of pension reform to reduce public debt, the top assignment for Guedes at the Finance Ministry. But the radical neo-liberal package Guedes laboured to prepare soon ran into two obstacles. On the one hand, Bolsonaro himself casually made clear that he was quite willing to ditch the centrepiece of Guedes's plan, a switch of the whole pension system from guaranteed public benefits to compulsory individual accounts, managed by private funds

---

2 Mediated through his sons, principally Eduardo, a stream of vituperations from the expatriate astrologer Olavo de Carvalho—Brazilian version of a seer of the Black Hundreds—has exerted a significant long-distance influence on this aspect of the regime.

along Chilean lines—not only a politically explosive proposal (average Chilean pensions falling below the minimum wage), but a fiscally hazardous scheme. On the other hand, Guedes's own lack of experience in navigating any measure—let alone one as sensitive as this, requiring a constitutional amendment—through Congress, coupled with the lack of any competent back-up from within the executive, left the shape of any such reform reverting to a legislature filled with deputies, conservative enough by any measure, but apprehensive of a backlash against too sharp an attack on privileged entitlements. Eventually, given business pressure, a neo-liberal pension reform was passed by the Lower House, and will no doubt be ratified by the Senate. Socially, its effect will hit the poor and precarious hardest; economically, its effect will be a cut in the revenues needed to finance the new system.[3]

Meanwhile all economic indicators point downwards, towards prolonged stagnation. Recovery from the recession of 2015–16, when GDP fell 7 per cent, was very weak in 2017–18, at no more than 1.1 per cent a year, as public spending was slashed, and consumption flatlined. Worse was to come in the first quarter of 2019, when far from getting a Bolsonaro bounce, the economy contracted by 0.2 per cent, and investment—despite the lowest interest rates since re-democratization—fell by 1.7 per cent for lack of effective demand, depressed by fiscal austerity at home and the retreat of commodity markets abroad.[4] Unaltered by

---

3 See Thomas Piketty, Marc Morgan, Amory Gethin and Pedro Paulo Zahluth Bastos, 'A quem interessa aumentar a desigualdade?', *Valor Económico*, 11 July 2019.

4 For the general economics of austerity from Dilma to Bolsonaro, see the authoritative work of Pedro Paulo Zahluth and his colleagues at the Centro de Estudos de Conjuntura e Política Econômica of the University of Campinas: latest bulletin, *A contração do PIB no primeiro trimestre e o risco de recessão em 2019*, May 2019.

Guedes, the neo-liberal medication of the crisis bequeathed by Temer has left unemployment at over 13 million, double the level before the crisis, and increased the number of Brazilians below the World Bank's minimalist definition of the poverty line by well over 7 million.[5] Capital itself has little reason for satisfaction with this performance; the masses, reasons for deepening despair. Without reversing it, the economic legitimation of the regime will vanish.

What of the judiciary, the second foot of the tripod? Had it not been for Lava Jato, Bolsonaro could never have come to power. Once elected, no move embellished the aura of his presidency more than his appointment of Sergio Moro as minister of justice. Personification of the battle against corruption, more popular in the country than the president himself, meanwhile supplying him with an ethically bullet-proof vest, Moro was widely seen as the most likely candidate to succeed Bolsonaro. The only question mark over his future seemed to be whether he would collide with Congress in pursuing further political malfeasance, or alternatively see his lustre dim if he allowed investigations to tail off once installed as minister. In the event, neither scenario materialized, both overtaken by a far more sensational one. In early June—six years almost to the day after he broke Snowden's revelation of Obama's worldwide empire of illegal surveillance— Glenn Greenwald and his colleagues at *The Intercept* started publishing exchanges between Moro and Dallagnol. These made it crystal-clear that, in defiance of the Constitution, judge and prosecutor had been colluding to secure Lula's imprisonment on evidence they knew to be weak, Moro directing operations of the prosecution in a case where he was supposed to be impartial.

---

5 See André Singer, 'Eterno retorno do pesadelo da pobreza', *Folha de S. Paulo*, 19 April 2019.

That much was, in truth, plain to see for anyone who cared to look, even without written evidence.[6] What the *Intercept* exchanges delivered was something beyond that, a brutal answer to the question posed by André Singer's description of the procedures of Lava Jato as at once 'republican' and 'factious': were they so in equal proportion? For not only did the messages show that the 2018 verdict against Lula was rigged, the judge who wrote it an eager party to the charge against him, and that the same judge was secretly in touch with what in the language of the Italian mafia would be called his 'referent' in the Supreme Court, Luiz Fux, reassuring Dallagnol of his ability to ensure its backing for their machinations with the memorable dictum (it could come from a novel by Sciascia): 'In Fux We Trust'.[7] They also proved, beyond any shadow of doubt, that the motivations of judge and prosecutors alike were political, extending to jeers at the PT, measures to ensure that Lula could give no interview to the press that might increase the PT's chances in the election, and—in a way, perhaps most damningly of all—measures to protect Cardoso, politically Lula's arch-enemy, from any risk that his own finances, lubricated too by Odebrecht, might be investigated. On being advised by Dallagnol that prosecutors in São Paulo who were apparently looking into these were probably just going through the motions to preserve an air of impartiality, Moro was still not pacified, finding it 'questionable' to 'offend someone whose support is important'. The ties binding the pool in Curitiba to the patriarch of the PSDB could not have been rendered more transparent.

Blithely waved away by Cardoso as 'a storm in a teacup',

---

6   See the conclusions above, pp. 159 ff.
7   Subsequently complemented, for a second referent on the Court, by a jubilant 'Fachin is ours' from Dallagnol.

the Vaza-Jato ('Car-Leak') revelations were a bombshell for less compromised liberal opinion. The reaction of three of the best-known columnists in the land, two of them famous for the ferocity of their attacks on the PT when it was in power, spoke volumes. Going from right to left within this bandwidth: in the words of Reinaldo Azevedo, the evidence of Vaza-Jato meant that 'if any law exists, the condemnation of Lula is null and void'; for Demétrio Magnoli, 'the collusion of Sergio Moro with the prosecutors' lay 'like a leaden cloud over our democracy', and now that it was exposed, 'any decent government would get rid of Moro without further ado. No such luck'; while for Elio Gaspari, Moro's continuation in office was 'an offence to morality, common sense and the laws of gravity', and he should resign forthwith; the political conduct of the pair in Curitiba resembled the sedition of the officers who had sought to overthrow Vargas in 1954.[8] Yet to expect such revulsion, however widespread or well-expressed, to bring Moro down, would be naive. Too much symbolic value had been invested in him for the Brazilian establishment of the hour—the president, the Supreme Court, Congress—to let him fall. But he was now damaged goods, no longer so much protecting Bolsonaro as protected by him. The judicial foot of the tripod has started to look as potentially shaky as the economic.

Within hours of Moro coming under fire, it was not the presidency that came to his defence. Bolsonaro, no doubt waiting to see what the fallout of Vaza-Jato would be, kept silent. It was the most powerful general in the regime who spoke out, and in

---

8   In chronological order—Gaspari: 'Moro, pede pra sair', *Folha de S. Paulo*, 12 June 2019; Magnoli: 'Não é sobre Lula ou Moro. A corrupção do sistema de Justiça não reprime a corrupção política', *Folha*, 15 June 2019; Azevedo: 'Havendo lei, condenação de Lula é nula', *Folha*, 21 June 2019.

terms that made starkly clear the political stake of the military in the common task, that had united officers and magistrates, of destroying Lula and ensuring that the PT could not win the elections of 2018. The intercepts, Augusto Heleno announced, 'seek to stain the image of Dr Sergio Moro, whose integrity and devotion to the fatherland are above suspicion'. Behind them were 'those who dominated the economic and political scene in Brazil in recent decades, and are now desperately using illegal means to try to prove that Justice punished them unjustly. They are going to be unmasked once more. The exchanges and accusations they are divulging confirm the honest and impartial work of those who had the law on their side. The judgment of the people will give these detractors the reply they deserve.' When Moro, to avoid the risk of an investigation of his conduct by the lower house of Congress, hastily presented himself to the upper house, where he was assured of a soft reception, Heleno was even more violently outspoken. He declared: 'Governed for twenty years by a veritable gang, the country was victim of a gigantic plunder of its resources, involving vast private firms and public enterprises, pension funds, administrators and politicians at all levels. Now some of the protagonists of this criminal project of power and illicit enrichment have brazenly participated in an inquisition of Minister Sergio Moro.'[9] Fellow officers in the regime chipped in with further affidavits to the same effect.

What such immediate intervention at a moment of crisis signals is that, in the tripod of forces sustaining Bolsonaro, the military are by far the most significant, supplying the regime with its most stable and powerful base. That, of course, was

9 'Ministros saem em defesa de Moro após vazamento de conversas com Dallagnol', *Estado de S.Paulo*, 10 June 2019; 'Heleno compara audiência de Moro no Senado a inquisição', *Estado de S. Paulo*, 20 June 2019.

always clear from the sheer number and weight of the government positions they occupy. Starting with Heleno at the top, in charge of Institutional Security, officers were handed control of the portfolios of Infrastructure, Science and Technology, Mines and Energy, and Defence. They were appointed comptroller-general, secretary-general to the presidency and secretary of government, not to speak of press secretary, Post Office director, aide to the president of the Supreme Court, etc. In all, no less than forty-five military appointments in the top two tiers of the administration. In comparative terms, Bolsonaro's regime numbers more ministers from the armed forces than ever served under the dictatorship: not just in Castelo Branco's government, at the outset of the dictatorship in 1964, but even in any of his military successors after the regime had hardened—Costa e Silva, Médici, Geisel and Figueiredo.[10]

What made this formidable resurrection and return, officers adorning the state en masse, politically possible? The answer, bitter as this may be, is that it was neither the Right nor the centre that accomplished this; neither the PFL/DEM nor the PSDB, neither the country's conservatives nor its neo-liberals. It was the Left, in the shape of the PT, which accomplished this and bears direct responsibility for the political rehabilitation and re-entry onto the political stage of the military. It did so oblivious of historical memory.

Scarcely over a year after the generals seized power in April 1964, the Brazilian dictatorship dispatched an expeditionary

---

10 Under the dictatorship, each of the three services had its own ministry. The chief of staff had ministerial rank, as did the head of the *Casa Militar*, and of the apparatus of internal surveillance and repression, the SNI. After democratization, these six positions were compressed to two—defence and institutional security. For the relevant figures, see 'Ministério terá mais militares do que em 1964', *Estado de S. Paulo*, 16 December 2018.

force to assist the US intervention to overthrow the constitutionalist authority headed by Francisco Caamaño in the Dominican Republic, feared as too radical by Washington. The counterrevolutionary force that took over the country was even put by the US under a Brazilian commander, the better to maintain the fiction of a pan-American response to the danger of communism in the hemisphere.

Some forty years later, another Brazilian expeditionary force landed on the same island, with much the same kind of mission, this time to cover the ouster of Jean-Bertrand Aristide in Haiti. The only political figure of modern times to enjoy a real following among the Haitian poor, Aristide was regarded in 2004 as too radical by the US and bundled into exile by Washington and its partners in Ottawa and Paris. Aristide, unlike Caamaño, presided over a government that by then—it was his third time in office—was guilty of intimidating its opponents, composed principally of military and economic legatees of Duvalier's brutal tyranny with far longer and worse records of violence, and no popular support of any kind. Amid mounting disorder, Aristide's inability to control the streets served as the pretext for an intervention whose motives lay elsewhere. For the US, Aristide had failed to be sufficiently business-friendly. For France, he had committed the unpardonable offence of demanding reparations for the crushing indemnity—some $21 billion in current values—that Haiti was forced to pay the restored Bourbon monarchy in 1825 as compensation for the emancipation of slaves decreed by the Haitian Revolution in 1793. It took the country over a century to pay off this staggering act of extortion.

Aristide was abducted by the US and despatched to exile on 28 February 2004. Within less than a week, Bush and Chirac made telephone calls to Lula, and Brazil announced it was sending troops to Haiti to command a UN peace-keeping force in the wake of his removal. What prompted the alacrity of its collusion with the trio of powers that came to be dubbed the Imperial Trident by Haitians?[11] The PT government sought to curry favour with the United States in the hope of Brazil being rewarded with a permanent seat on the UN Security Council, where France too held a veto power. Cynical in motive, naive in calculation—naturally, no such solatium was forthcoming—the dispatch of Brazilian troops merely served as 'the train-bearer of a coup', in Mario Sergio Conti's biting phrase.[12] The announced original cost was R$150 million, for a tour of six months. The actual expedition lasted thirteen years, and cost in the region of R$3 billion, rotating some 37,000 troops, half as many again as the expeditionary force sent to Italy in the Second World War. Its principal military feat? 'Operation Iron Fist', to cleanse the slum of Cité Soleil in Port-au-Prince, viewed as a stronghold of supporters of Aristide: 22,000 bullets and seventy-eight grenades fired, to kill seven members of a local gang; civilian casualties uncounted.[13]

Politically, the Trident kept its grip on Haiti throughout these years, staging another *coup de main* in 2010 to ensure that the presidency was in safe hands—one so blatant that Ricardo Seitenfus, the Brazilian special representative of the OAS in Haiti, himself a former emissary of Lula's government, could not

---

11   If the US and France took the lead in securing the Brazilian fig-leaf for the operation of the Trident, Canada was the first mover in preparations for its intervention in Haiti, convening a confidential meeting in Quebec as early as January 2003—no Haitians present—to discuss what action to take: see Yves Engler and Anthony Fenton, *Canada in Haiti: Waging War on the Poor Majority*, Vancouver 2006, pp. 41–4.

12   Mario Sergio Conti, 'O Haiti é aqui', *Folha de S. Paulo*, 26 January 2019: the outstanding historical reflection on the significance of the expedition.

13   Edwidge Danticat, 'A New Chapter for the Disastrous United Nations Mission in Haiti?', *New Yorker*, 19 October 2017.

contain his disgust and was fired for expressing it. In a blistering book-length retrospect of the record of the UN mission in Haiti, MINUSTAH, and of his country's role in it, he concluded: 'Brazil was not in Haiti to fight for democracy, still less for the interests of the majority of the population. It was there simply to further its international objectives ... Haiti was what it had always been, a mere means to a greater projection of Brazil on the international stage.'[14] After his departure, the US choice for a marionette in Port-au-Prince, the crooner-businessman Michel Martelly, was installed in the Presidential Palace by MINUSTAH on a vote of 4.3 per cent of the electorate, and went on to preside over a system of wholesale corruption, reviving the pitiless egoism of the country's traditional elites, steeped in the ways of Duvalier's dictatorship.[15] As for MINUSTAH, its parting legacy was the introduction of cholera into Haiti, leaving over

---

14 Ricardo Seitenfus, *Haiti: Dilemas e fracassos internacionais*, São Paulo 2014, pp. 330–1, 355. Among other things, his detailed account reveals the reasons why Urano Bacellar, the second of Brazil's generals to command MINUSTAH, committed suicide in Port-au-Prince in 2006, an episode over which Brasília sought to draw a veil (pp. 150–60).

15 See Robert Fatton Jr, *Haiti: Trapped in the Outer Periphery*, Boulder 2014, pp. 95, 121, 149—the third of this author's fine trilogy on his country, preceded by *Haiti's Predatory Republic* (2002) and *The Roots of Haitian Despotism* (2007), each unsparing in its depiction of the class from which, as he explains in a moving preface to the first, he himself comes: 'Born into the Haitian elite and having deep personal ties of affection to it, I am well acquainted with its behavior, mentality and prejudices ... [and] disturbingly familiar with the elite's profound contempt for *le peuple*. I know it fears democracy, and I know the hostility it harbors to the full exercise of universal suffrage.' Striking a rare note in scholarly writing of any kind, Fatton continues: 'Because I live in the privileged setting of academic life in the United States with the comfort that distance affords me, it is easy to pass moral judgment, but writing this book has been a profoundly painful and depressing intellectual and emotional process. It has entailed a difficult moral and political rupture with my own world, my own class': *Haiti's Predatory Republic*, p. xii.

8,000 dead and sickening 600,000 others, without the UN ever accepting responsibility for the victims.[16]

What would be the overall balance sheet of Brazil's descent on Haiti? After thirteen years, the Haitian masses were as trapped in misery as they were before Aristide, excluded from any say in their fate at the hands of their customary predators. Not even security, supposedly one of the immediate benefits the UN mission would bring, improved. Under its blue helmets, homicides doubled.[17] Gains for Brazil? Zero: the quest for a permanent seat at the Security Council, a waste of time. Elsewhere, the record of Lula's foreign policy was very different. Celso Amorim's memoir of his time as foreign minister is rightly proud of the independence of its later initiatives in the Middle East and at the WTO. Tellingly, however, it contains not one significant word on Brazil's intervention in Haiti—its silence, one must hope, a belated token of shame.[18] Beneficiaries of the expedition, however, there were. In the first place, of course, the United States, relieved of the onus of occupying Haiti, as it did for twenty years after 1914, and of having to guard Florida from too much floating black flotsam.[19] Far more momentously, however, the Brazilian armed forces, which supplied eleven successive commanders of the troops 'under the banner of the UN'; enjoyed

16 'Introduction' by the editors, in Robert Maguire and Scott Freeman (eds), *Who Owns Haiti? People, Power and Sovereignty*, Gainesville 2017, p. 5.

17 Fabiano Maisonnave and Danilo Verpa, 'Após 13 anos, Brasil deixa o Haiti entre paz frágil e miséria', *Folha de S. Paulo*, 27 August 2017.

18 In a work of some 500 pages, virtually the only reference to it is a passing allusion to 'the situation in Haiti, where under the command of a Brazilian general, and the banner of the United Nations, our soldiers were helping to maintain security': Celso Amorim, *Teerã, Ramalá e Doha: Memórias da política externa ativa e altiva*, São Paulo 2015, p. 182.

19 See Kenneth Maxwell's judgment, 'Brazil's Military Role in Haiti', *SLDinfo.com*, 19 June 2012.

wide-ranging modernization of their equipment (accounting for most of the cost of the expedition); learnt how to run tasks of a civilian administration; and came back to Brazil redeemed as the heroic guardians of an exemplary pacification. In celebration of their role, a florilegium was published under the auspices of the Ministry of Defence and a domesticated NGO, comprising one fulsome self-congratulation after another, its tone set by Floriano Peixoto, picked by Bolsonaro as his first secretary-general to the presidency. 'Brazil's military presence in Haiti for thirteen years', Peixoto explains, was 'an epic experience which fully realized all of the goals envisaged by its idealisers back in 2004'. Moreover, it was 'fundamental to point out' that to ensure this success, the country's soldiers drew on 'Brazil's previous military experience in 1965 and 1966 in the Dominican Republic, where we confirmed our role as a widely recognized international player'.[20] From Johnson to Bush, Castelo to Lula, servants of the same noble cause: how could they not be empowered to apply their dedication to tasks at home once again?

Colonization of the Bolsonaro regime by the military, returning in force some fifty years after a coup of which they remain proud, lends the intervening half-century of Brazilian history the form of a parabola. In 1964 they seized power to remove a president who was too willing to accept, as they saw it, radical changes in the social order. In 2018 they intervened to ensure that a president who was still too popular, as they saw it, after achieving less radical changes, could not be re-elected, and instead one of their own, by origin and outlook, came to power.

20 Floriano Peixoto, 'The Brazilian military experience in Haiti', in *Brazil's Participation in MINUSTAH 2004–2017: Perceptions, Lessons and Practices for Future Missions* [collection published in English], Rio de Janeiro 2017, p. 16. Peixoto was the fifth general to command the troops in Haiti.

The curve of a parabola need not be symmetrical. The toppling of Goulart and the blocking of Lula were distinct operations, the first requiring the exercise of violence, the second only the threat of it. If the language of imposition differed, prevention of 'subversion' in one case, of 'impunity' in the other, as acts of state the *pronunciamentos* of Mourão Filho in 1964 and Villas Bôas in 2018 were akin. The regimes to which they gave birth were not the same, each creatures of their context, products of contrasting historical circumstances. By the time of the second, there was no requirement for the tanks and torturers of the first, whatever Bolsonaro's nostalgia for them. Democracy had long been made safe for capital, and within the limits of the established social order, popular combativity was at a low ebb. Once installed, the new regime was more at risk from its own aporia than from any organized opposition to it.

There, in the anomaly of a former captain once nearly expelled from the army upending its hierarchy to command four-star generals, the head of the state has proved to be its destabilizer-in-chief. Bolsonaro's restless dismissals and reshuffles of his ministers—a rate of turnover faster and higher indeed than Trump's—have not spared even his military appointees. In the space of six months, he has abruptly fired two generals (Santos Cruz, Juarez Cunha), demoted a third (Peixoto), and co-opted a fourth (Ramos, unlike the others on active service) to handle relations with Congress; while relations with his decorated vice-president have visibly cooled. Professional discipline has so far prevailed, muting any public expressions of disaffection.[21] How long that will last is open to question.

There is also, potentially, a much more serious risk of an upset

---

21 In some cases, ties of friendship—Ramos was a roommate of Bolsonaro when they were cadets together in the Military Academy—come into play.

to the fragile equilibrium of the regime. Bolsonaro's original electoral base, and eventual political patrons, came from the army. But in the course of his entrenchment as an ideological firebrand in Rio, his closest connexions were with another apparatus of coercion, not federal but local, quite distinct from the army in its recruitment and *modus operandi*: the military police, a byword for corruption and criminality. There Bolsonaro and his sons wove former officers of this force—in retirement, the principal vectors of 'militias' preying on slums as drug-brokers and all-purpose enforcers—into their personal economic and political staff, while accumulating a quantum of real estate (thirteen properties to the value of some $4 million in the family) far beyond their means as deputies or assemblymen.[22]

One such ex-military policeman, Fabrício Queiroz, who served as chief of staff to Bolsonaro's eldest son Flávio, now federal senator for Rio, engaged in such blatantly suspect multiple cash deposits into a bankomat that an investigation of him was opened in early 2018, extended to the bank accounts of Flávio himself in 2019. On pretext of illness, Queiroz declined any questioning, and has since vanished. Also on Flávio's payroll were the mother and wife of another former military police officer, Adriano Nóbrega, once decorated by Bolsonaro himself. Nóbrega was later charged with murder, twice, and today is widely thought to be the leader of one of the most feared militia gangs in Rio, suspected of assassinating Marielle Franco. He too is on the lam, the authorities—naturally—unable to locate him. The explosive implications of this nexus for the president are

---

22 For particulars, see 'Patrimônio de Jair Bolsonaro e filhos se multiplica na política', *Folha de S. Paulo*, 7 January 2018. The salary of a federal deputy is around $100,000, lavish enough by international standards, but nowhere near enough to pile up a fortune of this kind.

plain. Likewise the pressures to suppress any risk of damage to him. The snail's pace of the investigation of Queiroz, which has now lasted for over 500 days without any charges being laid, and the unfindability of Nóbrega, speak for themselves. No one expects the minister of justice to be in any hurry to cast light on dark recesses of the ruler with whom he has thrown in his lot. Perhaps some brave spirit in the prosecutors' office in Rio will break ranks, but there is no counting on it.

What of public opinion? In the midst of prolonged economic recession and discredit of the political system, the main single driver of Bolsonaro's electoral victory was popular desire for change—whatever kind of change was on offer—at all costs. Disappointment soon followed. After six months in office, his positive approval ratings were the lowest of any first-term presidency since democratization, dropping from nearly half to a third of the population. Even among the better off and evangelicals, bastions of his support, there was a loss of enthusiasm. Principally responsible for the decline in his standing, polls showed, was not the absence of any economic recovery, or impasse of any particular reform, nor even the disjuncture between his rabid brand of identity politics and the trend of values of Brazilian society, where voters at large remain well to the left of him on moral as on socio-economic issues. Rather, what turned most of the disillusioned off was Bolsonaro's visible lack of preparation for government, his scatter-brained outbursts and want of gravitas, the general sense of a ruler adrift, lurching impulsively this way and that.[23]

Time may teach Bolsonaro elements of what public

---

23 See the findings of the IBOPE poll, 'Aprovação do governo Bolsonaro cai 15 pontos desde a posse' and 'Adequação ao cargo é vital para presidente recuperar confiança', *Folha de S. Paulo*, 20 March and 9 April 2019.

comportment as president requires, and of the need to compose with Congress if a neo-liberal agenda that meets the expectations of capital is to move smoothly forward. The possibility, however, cannot be excluded that, unwilling or unable to adjust his style, he goes the way of Collor, a scenario early ventilated in the media. For should the bonds of his clan with the underworld of Rio ever become too vividly exposed, it is not difficult to imagine another impeachment, disposing of him as an embarrassment to the new political order. In Congress the keeper of the keys to such a trial, Rodrigo Maia—son of a mayor of Rio repeatedly convicted of administrative dishonesty and son-in-law of one of the most flagrantly crooked oligarchs of the old PMDB, Wellington Moreira Franco, now under investigation along with Temer—is a worthy successor to Cunha: in manner more jovial, but in scruple infinitely flexible too, a figure quite capable of orchestrating Bolsonaro's removal from office. Would that be a deliverance for Brazil? Amid a chorus of praise for his moderation, already a basso continuo of *bien-pensant* commentary, General Hamilton Mourão, theorist of the virtues of a presidential 'auto-coup' in case of anarchy, would step up from the vice-presidency to become the country's new ruler. In the sum of things, the parabola of 1964 would have come to a yet more perfect landing.

INDEX